Money Untold Essence

The Real Rules to Reprogram Your Money Mindset and Escape Financial Mediocrity

The Hidden Architecture

Copyright © 2025 The Hidden Architecture
All rights reserved.

ISBN: 979-8-89860-326-7

No part of this publication may be reproduced, stored in a retrieval system, or transmitted in any form or by any means—electronic, mechanical, photocopying, recording, or otherwise—without the prior written permission of the author or publisher. All rights reserved under international and Pan-American copyright conventions.

Legal Notice: This publication is intended for personal use only. You may not modify, distribute, sell, use, quote, or paraphrase any part of this book without explicit consent from the author or publisher.

Disclaimer: The information contained within this book is provided for educational and entertainment purposes only. The author and publisher have made every effort to ensure the accuracy and completeness of the information presented. However, no warranties of any kind are expressed or implied. This book does not constitute legal, financial, medical, or professional advice. Readers should consult qualified professionals before applying any of the information contained herein. By reading this book, the reader agrees that the author and publisher shall not be held liable for any damages, losses, or liabilities caused directly or indirectly by the use or misuse of the information contained in this book, including but not limited to errors, omissions, or inaccuracies.

This is not advice. This is the architecture of freedom

Table of Contents

Introduction: Breaking the Code of Wealth 7

Part I. Breaking the Myths of Money 18
    Chapter 1: The Lies You've Been Sold About Money 20
    Chapter 2: Understanding the Real Game of Money 30

Part II. Rewiring Your Financial Mindset 40
    Chapter 3: The Psychology of Scarcity vs. Abundance 42
    Chapter 4: Value Creation as the Core of Wealth 52

Part III. Escaping the 9–5 Trap and Building Wealth 63
    Chapter 5: Breaking the 9–5 Trap 64
    Chapter 6: The Hidden Codes of the Wealthy 74

Part IV. Integrating the Hidden Codes 85
    Chapter 7: Mastering Cash Flow and Capital 87
    Chapter 8: Skill Acquisition and Monetization 97
    Chapter 9: The Invisible Forces of Money (Energy + Psychology) ... 107
    Chapter 10: Building Unfair Advantages 116
    Chapter 11: The New Rules of Financial Freedom 125
    Chapter 12: The Money Untold Essence Blueprint 134

Introduction: Breaking the Code of Wealth

Why Most Financial Advice Keeps You Stuck in Mediocrity

The shelves of every bookstore are lined with financial advice books promising to unlock the path to wealth. Podcasts, YouTube channels, and TikTok creators churn out endless tips about saving, investing, and budgeting. Yet despite this flood of information, most people still feel like they're standing in the same place. Their income barely stretches far enough. Their dreams of financial freedom remain distant. The reason isn't laziness or a lack of intelligence. The reason is that much of the advice people consume is built to keep them comfortable, not to set them free.

Mainstream financial guidance is designed around safety. It tells you to save ten percent of your income, cut back on lattes, contribute to your retirement fund, and wait patiently for decades. On the surface, it sounds responsible. But beneath it is a subtle message: stay where you are, play it safe, and hope that one day you will be rewarded. This advice might help you avoid disaster, but it will never propel you toward the kind of wealth that changes your life.

The Problem with "Play It Safe"

Traditional advice assumes the goal is to avoid failure rather than pursue extraordinary success. It encourages people to protect what little they have, rather than expand what they could build. By prioritizing security above growth, this advice often discourages risk in any form. The result is predictable: people stay locked in the same income brackets, living paycheck to paycheck, while believing they are doing everything right.

Psychologist Daniel Kahneman's research on loss aversion illustrates why this happens. His studies revealed that humans fear losing money twice as much as they enjoy gaining it. When combined with financial advice that emphasizes security, this fear keeps people from ever making moves that could lead to significant change. They cling to predictable routines because those routines feel safer, even if they guarantee mediocrity.

The Illusion of Progress

Another reason mainstream advice fails is that it often creates the illusion of movement without real transformation. People are told to build detailed budgets, track every expense, and cut back on pleasures like dining out or small luxuries. This can feel productive — checking off tasks and seeing small savings pile up. Yet the bigger picture remains unchanged. Earning potential doesn't grow. Skills that create leverage are never developed. The focus stays on shrinking life rather than expanding it.
This pattern can be comforting. It gives a sense of control in a chaotic financial world. But comfort is rarely where growth happens. Many realize years later that they've been perfecting the art of living small rather than mastering the ability to create more.

Why This Advice Persists

If traditional advice is so limited, why is it everywhere? The truth is uncomfortable: mediocrity is profitable. Banks, employers, and even governments benefit when people stay predictable. Saving accounts generate fees. Stable employees keep companies running. Consumers focused on cutting back rarely question deeper systems of wealth creation. The mainstream narrative keeps people busy but uninformed.
There is also a cultural factor. Many societies romanticize frugality as a virtue while quietly shaming ambition. Wanting more is seen as greedy rather than visionary. People who break away from conventional paths are often criticized until they succeed, at which point their story is retold as inspiring — but without any real discussion of the bold moves that got them there.
What separates those who quietly build extraordinary wealth is not the willingness to follow rules more strictly, but the courage to question the rules altogether. They look at the same world most people see and notice the gaps, the inefficiencies, the opportunities hiding in plain sight. Where traditional advice says "save what you can," they ask, "how can I create more?" Where others settle for stability, they learn to think in terms of leverage — how time, skills, and capital can multiply instead of merely accumulate.

This difference begins with mindset but doesn't end there. Belief alone won't make you wealthy, yet belief is the lens through which every financial decision is made. If you believe money is scarce, you will act in ways that confirm that scarcity: avoiding risks, underpricing your skills, clinging to comfort. If you believe money is abundant and that value can be created rather than merely traded, your choices change. You look for opportunities to serve more people, to solve bigger problems, and to expand your reach. That shift may sound subtle, but it transforms the trajectory of your life.

The problem is that mainstream financial advice rarely addresses this deeper layer. It treats symptoms rather than causes. It tells you how to allocate a paycheck without ever questioning why your earning potential is capped in the first place. It offers formulas for saving on groceries without teaching you how to build assets that outpace inflation. This is why people can follow every piece of advice they are given — cut spending, pay off debt, save diligently — and still feel like they are running in circles. They are optimizing a flawed system rather than redesigning it.

There is also a hidden psychological cost. When you follow restrictive advice for long enough, you begin to internalize the idea that wealth is only for others. You accept mediocrity as inevitable because you rarely see anyone in your immediate circle breaking free from it. The advice you've been given reinforces this belief by focusing on limitation rather than expansion. Over time, this belief hardens into identity: "I am someone who survives, not someone who thrives." Without realizing it, you've built a mental ceiling that keeps you where you are.

Breaking this cycle begins with understanding that financial freedom requires both protection and creation. Protection matters — avoiding unnecessary debt, managing expenses, building a safety net — but it cannot be the whole plan. At some point, you must shift focus from protecting pennies to producing value. That means learning skills that command higher income, finding leverage through systems or partnerships, and aligning your work with opportunities that grow rather than deplete you.

Practical wealth building also demands a longer view. Research on delayed gratification, like Walter Mischel's marshmallow experiments, showed that those who can trade short-term comfort for future rewards tend to achieve far greater outcomes in every area of life. This principle applies directly to money. When you stop seeking instant results and start building assets and skills that compound over time, you step onto a path most people never find. Patience, combined with strategic action, quietly outperforms frantic hustle.

None of this is about reckless risk-taking or chasing unrealistic fantasies. It's about shifting from reactive habits to intentional design. The wealthy are not playing a different game because they were handed secret opportunities. They are playing a different game because they learned to think differently about value, risk, and growth. They stepped away from advice that kept them small and started seeking principles that expanded what was possible. As you move deeper into this book, keep questioning the assumptions you've carried about money. Ask who benefits from you staying where you are. Consider what beliefs you've inherited about work, wealth, and worth — and whether those beliefs still serve you. The chapters ahead will not only reveal the real rules but will give you tools to apply them, replacing confusion and mediocrity with clarity and momentum. This is the turning point where financial advice stops being a script you follow and becomes a framework you create for yourself.

The Hidden Patterns Behind Quiet Wealth (Beyond Hustle Culture)

When most people think of wealth, they imagine relentless hustle. Long nights, constant networking, a life consumed by work. Social media has glorified this image of success, painting it as the only path to financial freedom. Yet behind the scenes, a very different pattern plays out. The truly wealthy — especially those who quietly accumulate fortune rather than flaunt it — rarely follow the grind-until-you-drop approach. Their wealth grows in ways that look subtle from the outside but are deliberate and structured at the core.

The Illusion of Hustle

Hustle culture thrives on visibility. It rewards people who appear busy, who share their sacrifices, and who broadcast their every move. The message is simple: more hours equals more success. But this mindset can be a trap. Constant activity can create the illusion of progress while masking the lack of real leverage. Working more hours may raise income in the short term, but without systems or scalable strategies, it simply trades time for money. The quiet wealthy understand this distinction. They may work hard, but their focus is on positioning, not perpetual motion. Instead of asking, "How can I work more?" they ask, "How can I make this work without me?" This question leads to building assets — businesses, investments, intellectual property — that generate income whether or not they are actively grinding.

The Shift from Effort to Leverage

At the heart of quiet wealth is a mindset shift: effort alone is never enough. The people who quietly escape financial mediocrity learn to use leverage. This could mean leveraging capital, skills, networks, or technology. It is about multiplying results without multiplying effort.

Consider someone who spends years mastering a rare skill. At first, the income may look similar to any other career path. But over time, that skill becomes highly valuable and scalable — allowing them to command higher rates, train others, or build products around their expertise. The same principle applies to financial capital: rather than hoarding savings in a low-yield account, they deploy it into investments that grow on their own. This quiet compounding is what creates long-term stability and eventual abundance.

The Role of Patience and Compounding

Quiet wealth rarely happens fast, but it often accelerates after years of consistent alignment. Compounding is the hidden force at play — small, repeated actions that build exponential results over time. While hustle culture burns energy in short sprints, compounding builds quietly in the background.

This principle applies to both money and skills. A modest investment, consistently added to and wisely managed, becomes significant over decades. Likewise, learning and stacking complementary skills — marketing with design, finance with leadership, coding with communication — eventually creates unique combinations that are hard to replicate and highly rewarded.

Why Quiet Wealth Stays Quiet

Those who build wealth this way often avoid the spotlight. They are not chasing social validation or external applause; their focus is freedom and autonomy. Visibility can even become a liability, drawing unwanted attention or pressure. Instead of projecting success, they quietly structure their lives to work for them, building safety nets and opportunities without needing to prove anything to anyone.

This subtle approach is powerful precisely because it looks unremarkable from the outside. While others are chasing trends or broadcasting hustle, these individuals are quietly stacking assets, deepening skills, and positioning themselves to win over the long term.

One of the most striking features of people who quietly accumulate wealth is their ability to detach from short-term status markers. They are not driven by showing off a lifestyle but by designing one that feels sustainable and free from constant financial pressure. This shift away from outward appearances allows them to direct energy into systems that grow in the background rather than performative busyness that exhausts them.

A pattern that emerges consistently is their focus on ownership rather than employment. While mainstream advice prioritizes job security and steady paychecks, those who build quiet wealth deliberately position themselves on the other side of that equation. They acquire equity in businesses, create intellectual property, or invest in appreciating assets. Even when they begin with traditional employment, they use it as a stepping stone, saving aggressively not to stockpile cash but to redeploy it into ventures or investments that will later free them from relying on a single source of income.

Another pattern is the deliberate cultivation of asymmetry in decision-making. Instead of taking equal risks for equal rewards, they seek opportunities where the potential upside far outweighs the downside. This principle is often misunderstood because it does not necessarily mean taking extreme risks; rather, it means making calculated moves where the cost of failure is manageable but the payoff could be transformative. A modest investment in developing a unique skill, a side project that can scale, or a carefully chosen business partnership can all become high-upside plays that look almost invisible to the outside world.

Patience plays a critical role in this approach. Those who chase quick wins often find themselves trapped in cycles of burnout and disappointment. In contrast, quiet wealth builders understand that compounding takes time to reveal its results. They stay committed to consistent contributions, whether in learning, investing, or building systems, trusting that the long-term trajectory matters more than immediate gratification. This patience allows them to avoid the reactive decision-making that often comes from comparing themselves to others or trying to "catch up" to visible success stories.

Their financial behavior also reflects an uncommon level of intentionality. They do not view budgeting or investing as chores but as strategic choices aligned with a bigger vision. Every dollar has a purpose, whether it is being directed toward acquiring assets, funding new skills, or building reserves for future moves. This intentionality is what allows them to quietly accumulate advantages while others spend impulsively or chase short-lived trends.

It is worth noting that this path requires a mindset of continuous learning. The landscape of opportunities changes, industries evolve, and the tools available for building wealth expand over time. The quiet wealthy remain curious and adaptive, studying patterns others ignore and adjusting their strategies without broadcasting every move. This commitment to learning ensures that they are rarely blindsided by shifts in the economy or marketplace.

These patterns, though subtle, create a powerful compounding effect. Small, intentional choices made consistently over years build a level of financial stability and freedom that is invisible until it becomes undeniable. It is the opposite of hustle culture's frantic energy. Instead of constantly proving themselves, they quietly design lives that work in their favor, day after day, year after year. Understanding these patterns is the first step toward adopting them — and once you see them clearly, it becomes impossible to return to the noisy, exhausting grind that most people mistake for progress.

How This Book Rewires Both Mindset and Action to Unlock Your Potential

Lasting financial change begins in the mind, but it cannot stop there. The right mindset opens the door, yet without matching action, it is only potential energy. On the other hand, action without the right beliefs behind it often leads to burnout or choices that sabotage long-term goals. The purpose of this book is to align both — to reshape how you see money and teach you how to act on that new understanding in ways that create lasting freedom.

Rewriting the Internal Blueprint

Every financial decision you make is filtered through beliefs you may not even know you hold. These beliefs often come from family, culture, or past experiences. Some people grow up hearing that money is scarce and must be clung to tightly. Others learn that wealth is something other people have, not something attainable for them. These unexamined scripts operate quietly, influencing choices about spending, saving, and even self-worth.

This book challenges those scripts head-on. Through examples, reflection prompts, and practical strategies, you will learn to identify the specific beliefs that have shaped your relationship with money. More importantly, you will learn how to replace them with new ones rooted in value creation and abundance rather than fear or limitation. When your mental framework shifts, opportunities that once felt invisible suddenly become clear, and decisions that once felt impossible become second nature.

Moving Beyond Surface-Level Advice

Most financial advice focuses on surface-level fixes: cut back on expenses, create a budget, find a side hustle. While these tactics can help temporarily, they do not address why you make certain choices in the first place. If you have ever stuck to a budget for a few months only to revert to old habits, you already know that tactics alone are not enough. Something deeper must change.

The rewiring process this book offers goes beneath tactics to the drivers behind them. It does not just tell you what to do; it helps you understand why it matters and how to make it sustainable. Instead of relying on willpower, you will learn to set up your environment, routines, and systems so that good decisions become effortless. The result is financial growth that compounds quietly without constant struggle.

From Mindset to Measurable Action

Shifting your perspective is only half the journey. Once you begin to think differently about money, you must act differently too. This book equips you with specific frameworks for building and managing wealth: identifying opportunities for leverage, stacking skills that multiply income, and creating systems that work even when you are not actively involved. These are not quick fixes; they are habits and structures designed to last.

Research on behavior change, such as that by Carol Dweck on growth mindset, shows that people who believe they can develop new abilities are far more likely to persist through challenges and reach higher levels of achievement. When you combine that belief with clear, repeatable steps, transformation becomes not just possible but predictable.

The chapters ahead are built to guide you through this dual transformation — internal and external — so that by the end of the book you are not only thinking differently about wealth but living differently too.

You will also notice that the approach here does not separate personal growth from financial growth. The two are inseparable. If you attempt to change your financial habits without addressing the beliefs that drive them, the change will not last. And if you focus only on positive thinking without developing tangible skills or systems, you will stay stuck in the same circumstances. This book is structured so that each mindset shift naturally leads into a matching action step, allowing you to see results quickly and build confidence as you progress.

This integration is what creates momentum. When you act on a new belief and see real outcomes — a bill paid off faster, a skill monetized, a new income stream started — the experience reinforces the belief itself. That reinforcement is what locks the change in place. Over time, what once felt difficult begins to feel natural. What once seemed unrealistic becomes part of your daily reality. This is how genuine transformation happens: belief fuels action, and action strengthens belief, creating a cycle that grows stronger with each step forward.

The rewiring process also accounts for the psychological traps that keep many people from lasting change. One of the most common is the false sense of urgency created by hustle culture. Constant busyness tricks people into feeling productive even when their efforts are scattered and unaligned. Here, you will learn to slow down enough to focus on what actually compounds — high-value actions that, while less dramatic, quietly shape a future of financial independence. Understanding which actions truly move the needle will save you years of wasted energy.

Another trap this book helps you escape is the passive mindset encouraged by conventional financial narratives. Many are told that wealth comes from waiting: work hard for decades, save diligently, and eventually you will retire comfortably. The reality is that waiting alone rarely leads to freedom. Building wealth requires designing systems that work on multiple levels — from how you manage income and assets to how you continue to grow skills that increase earning power. This is where mindset and action meet: your perspective determines how you see opportunities, and your actions determine how you capitalize on them.

The tools in these chapters are designed to be adaptable rather than prescriptive. Not everyone will follow the same path or pursue the same type of opportunities. Some may focus on entrepreneurship, others on high-value careers or investments. The principles, however, remain constant: create value, use leverage wisely, and build habits that support sustainable growth. By the end, you will have a framework that applies to any path you choose, rooted in clear thinking and deliberate practice.

What makes this especially powerful is how it shifts the measure of success. Instead of chasing arbitrary financial milestones, you will learn to evaluate progress by freedom, stability, and alignment with your values. This shift not only reduces stress but also prevents the endless cycle of "more is never enough" that traps so many ambitious people. The goal is not just to accumulate money but to build a life where money serves you rather than controls you.

As you move forward, each concept will build on the last, gradually rewiring both your internal beliefs and your external habits. The end result is a system you understand deeply, one that continues to work long after the excitement of reading a new book fades. This is how lasting wealth is created — quietly, steadily, and on your terms.

Part I. Breaking the Myths of Money

Every belief you hold about money shapes how you earn it, spend it, and either grow or lose it. The problem is that most of those beliefs are inherited rather than chosen. They come from parents who struggled, teachers who emphasized security over ambition, and a culture that glorifies the grind but hides the real rules of wealth creation. By the time most people start managing their own finances, they are following an invisible script they never wrote.

This script is filled with myths. Some are comforting — work hard, stay patient, and one day you will be rewarded. Others are quietly limiting — success is for the lucky few, and wanting more makes you selfish. Even the advice you've been told is "responsible" can keep you stuck, convincing you that shrinking your dreams is the same as being wise. These myths are so widespread that they often go unquestioned. Yet when you look closely at those who have quietly built lasting wealth, you see something different. They do not follow these rules. They do not even play the same game.

Breaking these myths is the first step to real freedom. It requires unlearning, which can feel uncomfortable at first. You may realize that strategies you believed were safe have actually kept you in place. You may discover that some sacrifices you were praised for making have cost you opportunities you didn't know existed. This is not about blaming yourself or anyone else. It is about seeing clearly for the first time. Once you do, you can start replacing these myths with principles that actually work.

This part of the book will reveal the illusions that keep most people in financial mediocrity. It will show why conventional wisdom about hard work, stability, and cautious planning can limit your potential rather than unlock it. More importantly, it will begin introducing the hidden patterns of those who operate differently — the quiet wealthy who understand value, leverage, and long-term positioning in ways mainstream advice never teaches. These insights are not about shortcuts or reckless risks. They are about aligning your thinking with reality and positioning yourself to take advantage of opportunities most people cannot even see.

By the end of this section, you will have a new lens for everything you thought you knew about money. You will recognize why the old rules failed and why following them leads to predictable outcomes that no longer serve you. With that clarity, you will be ready to step into the frameworks and strategies that form the foundation for real financial transformation.

Chapter 1: The Lies You've Been Sold About Money

The Myth of Hard Work Alone

One of the most persistent ideas about money is that if you work hard enough, success will eventually follow. From childhood, most people are taught to value effort above all else. Work hard at school, work hard at your job, work hard to save. This message is repeated so often that it feels unquestionable. Yet when you look around, it becomes clear that effort alone does not explain why some people thrive financially while others remain stuck. Many of the hardest-working individuals are not the wealthiest. In fact, some of the wealthiest people have lives that do not look like hard work at all.

This is not to suggest that hard work has no value. Consistency and discipline matter, and laziness rarely leads to progress. The problem lies in believing that hard work is the only factor that matters. That belief blinds you to the other forces that shape wealth: leverage, strategy, timing, and mindset. Without these elements, effort becomes a treadmill — constant motion without meaningful advancement.

Why Effort Alone Fails

Hard work feels safe because it is within your control. You can always add more hours, push yourself harder, or sacrifice more in the name of progress. This approach seems noble, but it can trap you in a cycle of exhaustion with limited returns. If every dollar you earn requires more of your time, your income will always be capped by the number of hours you can work. The harder you push, the more you sacrifice, yet the ceiling remains.

Research on income mobility consistently shows that opportunity and strategy play larger roles in wealth creation than effort alone. In his work on behavioral economics, Daniel Kahneman observed that people often underestimate the role of luck and systems while overestimating the impact of personal effort. This is why two individuals can work equally hard in different contexts and achieve vastly different results. One might spend years grinding at a low-wage job, while another leverages a high-value skill or a scalable system and builds exponential income.

The Cultural Weight of the Work Ethic

The belief in hard work as the ultimate answer is deeply cultural. In many societies, it is tied to morality: those who work hard are "good" and those who struggle must not be trying enough. This narrative can keep people loyal to systems that do not reward them. They feel obligated to endure long hours in jobs that offer no growth, convinced that persistence alone will eventually pay off. It rarely does.

Hustle culture has amplified this narrative, equating exhaustion with achievement. Social media glorifies endless grinding, late nights, and constant busyness as proof of dedication. Yet what this culture rarely shows is the quiet cost: burnout, missed opportunities for leverage, and the illusion of progress without meaningful financial change.

The Missing Ingredient: Leverage

Those who escape mediocrity understand that effort is only the starting point. They look for ways to multiply their effort so that one hour of work creates results that last long after that hour is over. This could mean building a product once and selling it repeatedly, acquiring assets that generate income on their own, or creating systems that allow others to contribute to their vision. Hard work may initiate these opportunities, but leverage is what turns them into lasting wealth.

The difference is not always obvious from the outside. Quiet wealth often grows behind the scenes, without dramatic displays of hustle. The people building it may appear to work less, but what they are really doing is directing their energy toward activities that scale rather than simply intensify. Their success comes from focus, not frantic effort.

Leverage does not eliminate effort, but it ensures the energy you invest produces results far beyond what direct labor alone could create. A person working seventy hours a week at a job with no equity or scalable outcomes may be praised for their dedication but will always be limited by the clock. In contrast, someone who spends the same number of hours building an asset — whether that is a small business, a book of clients, or a portfolio of investments — can eventually earn income without trading more time for it. This is the difference between linear returns and exponential ones.

The transition from pure effort to leveraged action often begins with a shift in how value is perceived. Most people equate value with time: an hour of work equals an hour of pay. Those who break out of mediocrity view value differently. They ask what results their work produces, not how many hours they put in. This mindset shift allows them to prioritize learning skills that command higher value, finding problems worth solving, and building systems that multiply their contribution. Once this becomes second nature, it no longer feels like abandoning hard work but rather elevating it to a level where every hour builds toward something enduring.

Quiet wealth builders also understand that their energy and attention are finite. By acknowledging this, they become selective about where to apply effort. Instead of scattering focus across dozens of low-impact tasks, they double down on actions that create leverage. This might mean declining overtime to study a new skill, redirecting spare income toward an asset instead of consumer goods, or carefully choosing a single side project with long-term potential rather than chasing multiple short-lived opportunities. The principle is simple: the highest return comes from compounding focus, not just compounding hours.

There is also a psychological release that comes with abandoning the myth of hard work alone. When you stop measuring your worth by how busy you are, you give yourself permission to think strategically. This space allows creativity to emerge, revealing solutions that cannot be found when you are constantly reacting to the demands of the day. Many breakthroughs in wealth-building come not from grinding harder but from stepping back, observing patterns, and asking better questions about how to create impact. Understanding this myth does not mean rejecting discipline or avoiding effort. It means recognizing that effort is most powerful when paired with intention. Working hard at the wrong things, no matter how noble it feels, only deepens frustration. Working hard at the right things, in ways that scale, creates a path toward freedom. This book will return to this principle repeatedly, because every strategy you learn — from building skills to positioning capital — depends on escaping the trap of equating busyness with progress.

As you read forward, begin examining your own relationship with effort. Ask where your energy currently flows and whether it leads to outcomes that build over time or simply reset every morning. Consider how you might direct even a portion of that effort toward actions that create leverage, whether through skills, networks, or assets. This single shift can transform not only your finances but also your quality of life, allowing you to work from clarity rather than compulsion. The chapters that follow will help you make this transition step by step, showing how hard work, when paired with the right frameworks, can finally deliver the freedom you have been seeking.

The Illusion of Stability

One of the most powerful forces keeping people in financial mediocrity is the belief that stability equals security. The promise of a steady paycheck, health benefits, and predictable routines creates a sense of safety that feels comforting. Society reinforces this at every level, praising those who "settle down" with reliable employment and consistent income. On the surface, this appears wise and responsible. But when examined closely, this notion of stability is often fragile, built on assumptions that can unravel with a single unexpected event.

The False Safety of Predictable Income

A steady job feels secure because it provides a guaranteed monthly paycheck. This predictability can be reassuring, especially for those who have grown up equating financial consistency with safety. Yet history shows how easily this kind of stability can vanish. Companies restructure, industries shift, economies crash. Layoffs, mergers, or even technological disruptions can eliminate roles overnight, leaving workers scrambling without warning. The very stability people rely on is contingent on factors beyond their control.

This false safety can create complacency. When income feels guaranteed, there is little incentive to think beyond the next paycheck or to prepare for the possibility of disruption. The result is a subtle but dangerous dependence — not on one's skills or assets, but on an employer's willingness to keep paying. True security comes from adaptability and ownership, not from a paycheck that can disappear at any time.

Why Stability Feels So Attractive

The pull of stability is rooted in psychology. Human beings are wired to avoid uncertainty. Predictable routines reduce anxiety and create the impression of control. This is why many people stay in jobs they dislike or accept limited growth opportunities: the discomfort of change feels riskier than the quiet dissatisfaction of staying put. In behavioral economics, this tendency is called "status quo bias" — the preference for the familiar, even when better options exist.

Society reinforces this bias. From a young age, people are told that the safest path is to get a good job, stay loyal, and climb the ladder. This narrative worked in past generations when pensions, long-term employment, and stable economies were the norm. But today's world is different. The speed of change in technology and global markets means that what feels stable today may be obsolete tomorrow.

The Cost of Believing the Illusion

Clinging to the illusion of stability often prevents people from building true financial resilience. They delay learning high-value skills, investing in assets, or exploring alternative income streams because they feel no urgency to do so. When disruption inevitably arrives — whether through layoffs, industry changes, or personal circumstances — they realize too late that they have no safety net outside their paycheck.

This illusion also shapes spending habits. Many assume that consistent income justifies fixed expenses like mortgages, car payments, or lifestyle upgrades. As income grows, so does spending, leaving little room for savings or investment. The result is a life that looks stable on the outside but is extremely vulnerable beneath the surface.

True security begins when you shift focus from protecting what you have to creating something that can grow independently of your job or employer. This does not necessarily mean quitting immediately or taking reckless risks. It means gradually building a foundation of assets, skills, and systems that give you options. Options are what transform financial anxiety into confidence. When income does not rely on a single source, the fear of sudden change loses its grip.

One way to create this foundation is by prioritizing ownership. This could be equity in a business you build, intellectual property you develop, or investments that generate passive returns. Ownership removes the dependence on an external decision-maker to determine your future. Even small steps toward ownership compound over time, eventually replacing the need for external stability with a form of security that cannot be taken away as easily.

Another critical shift is recognizing that adaptability is more valuable than predictability. The quiet wealthy excel at scanning for opportunities and adjusting when conditions change. They stay aware of trends in technology, markets, and industries, positioning themselves ahead of shifts instead of being caught off guard by them. This mindset removes the illusion that stability must mean staying the same. Instead, it reframes stability as the ability to remain grounded regardless of external changes.

The financial habits that support true security are also different from those built on the illusion of stability. Rather than tying spending to a consistent paycheck, they design their lives to live below their means even as income grows. Surplus resources are directed into building assets, reducing liabilities, and creating buffers that allow flexibility when unexpected events occur. This discipline is not about deprivation but about freedom — the ability to make decisions without being trapped by obligations or fear.

Psychologically, letting go of the illusion of stability can be uncomfortable. It challenges deeply ingrained beliefs about what it means to be responsible. It requires confronting the reality that the systems people rely on — jobs, benefits, pensions — are often not as unshakable as they seem. But once this discomfort is faced, it opens the door to a new kind of peace: the confidence that comes from building security on your own terms rather than waiting for someone else to provide it.

Understanding this shift sets the stage for everything that follows in this book. The strategies ahead are not about reckless leaps but about deliberate moves toward independence and control. They will show you how to recognize fragile systems, build resilience through value creation, and step into opportunities that others overlook because they are clinging to routines that no longer serve them. Breaking free from the illusion of stability is not just a financial decision but a mental one, and it marks the beginning of genuine wealth-building that lasts.

Who Benefits From Your Financial Blind Spots

Most people assume their financial struggles are personal failings: a lack of discipline, bad decisions, or simply bad luck. While individual choices matter, what often goes unseen is how the financial system is structured to take advantage of blind spots in the way people think and behave with money. These blind spots are not random. They are understood and exploited by corporations, marketers, and even governments. The result is a cycle where individuals unknowingly play a role in enriching others at their own expense.

How Blind Spots Are Created

Blind spots form when there is a gap between how money actually works and how people believe it works. From early education to cultural narratives, most people are taught only the basics of earning and spending, not the deeper mechanics of value creation, leverage, or long-term wealth. This lack of understanding leaves room for myths and half-truths to take root. Once in place, these beliefs influence every financial decision, often leading people to prioritize short-term comfort over long-term security.

Consider how little formal education most people receive about taxes, investing, or debt management. Instead of learning how to make systems work in their favor, they are left to navigate complex financial landscapes on their own. Meanwhile, those who design these systems — corporations, lenders, and policymakers — operate with far more information and resources. They understand human behavior well enough to predict how most people will act and position themselves to profit from it.

Who Gains From the Confusion

Credit card companies are a clear example. Their profits depend on people carrying balances and paying interest. They know many will overspend due to emotional triggers or a lack of understanding about compound interest. Rather than helping customers avoid debt, they design rewards programs and minimum payment options that encourage ongoing borrowing. Banks and lenders operate similarly, earning billions from overdraft fees, late payments, and penalties that thrive on poor financial habits.

Retailers and marketers also benefit from blind spots, particularly around impulse buying and lifestyle inflation. Advertising is crafted to tap into psychological triggers — scarcity, social proof, fear of missing out — encouraging people to spend more than they intend. This is not accidental. Entire industries exist to influence behavior in ways that prioritize consumption over savings or investment. The result is a population that feels perpetually behind, always chasing the next purchase that promises happiness but rarely delivers it.

Even employers can benefit from financial blind spots. When workers believe job stability is the only path to security, they are less likely to negotiate salaries, pursue better opportunities, or build independent income streams. This loyalty serves companies well, keeping labor costs predictable and turnover low, but it often leaves individuals underpaid and overextended.

The moment you recognize these dynamics, the power begins to shift. Awareness is not about paranoia but about clarity. It allows you to see patterns you once accepted as normal and begin questioning whether they serve you or someone else. When you realize that certain systems profit from your inaction or lack of knowledge, you can make deliberate moves to reclaim control.

One of the most effective ways to dismantle these blind spots is to identify where your money habits feel automatic. Automatic behaviors are often clues to unseen influences. Do you find yourself upgrading your lifestyle as soon as income rises, without planning for long-term goals? Are you more focused on credit card rewards than on avoiding the interest that quietly cancels them out? Do you rely entirely on your paycheck without building any assets that can sustain you if that paycheck disappears? These are signals that you may be participating in patterns that benefit others more than they benefit you.

Changing these patterns requires replacing reactive decisions with intentional ones. Rather than accepting financial products or cultural expectations at face value, ask what incentives lie behind them. When a company offers "buy now, pay later" financing, consider who profits from that arrangement. When you receive advice to stay loyal to a single employer for security, ask who gains most from your loyalty. This level of questioning does not lead to cynicism; it leads to informed choices.

Another important step is shifting from being a consumer to being a creator. Blind spots are often exploited because people are positioned solely as buyers rather than owners. The more you understand how value is created and captured, the easier it becomes to step onto the other side of the equation. This might mean learning skills that allow you to sell your expertise rather than only your time, building a side business that grows into an asset, or investing in ventures where your money works on your behalf. The goal is not to avoid spending altogether but to ensure that your spending aligns with your values and future plans rather than with someone else's marketing agenda.

Breaking free from financial blind spots also involves accepting that systems will not change for you. Corporations will continue to optimize for profit, advertisers will continue to leverage psychology, and employers will continue to prioritize their own sustainability. Waiting for the world to become fairer is not a strategy. Taking personal responsibility for seeing and navigating these realities is. This is what separates those who quietly build wealth from those who remain caught in cycles of reaction and regret.

Once you learn to recognize these hidden influences, you gain the ability to make choices that others overlook. You start seeking opportunities where others only see obstacles, questioning offers that others accept without thought, and prioritizing growth that goes beyond the next paycheck. This shift in perspective is not instant, but it compounds over time, creating a foundation of awareness and resilience that protects you from being manipulated by systems designed to profit from confusion. It is this level of clarity that prepares you for the deeper strategies ahead, where the real work of building quiet wealth begins.

Chapter 2: Understanding the Real Game of Money

The Four Money Games People Play

Most people think of money as one single game. You work, you earn, you spend, and hopefully you save a little along the way. But in reality, people are playing very different games, often without realizing it. These games are defined not just by income but by how individuals approach risk, value, and leverage. Understanding these four games is essential because it shows you why some people remain stuck while others quietly accelerate toward freedom. Once you recognize which game you are playing — and which game you should be playing — your entire strategy changes.

The Survival Game

The first and most common game is survival. In this game, people focus on covering basic expenses: rent, food, transportation, and bills. The goal is not wealth but simply getting through the month without falling behind. For many, this game is relentless. Paychecks are spent almost as soon as they arrive, and emergencies can quickly spiral into debt. Survival players often live with constant stress because there is no margin for error.

What keeps people trapped in the survival game is the belief that working harder will eventually lead to escape. While increased effort can temporarily improve circumstances, it rarely creates lasting change. Without access to higher-value skills, financial literacy, or opportunities for leverage, hard work alone becomes a cycle of running faster on the same treadmill. The focus stays on income rather than on building assets that could eventually break the pattern.

The Comfort Game

The second game is comfort. People in this stage have moved beyond basic survival and earn enough to cover their needs with some room for discretionary spending. Comfort players often experience a sense of relief compared to survival, which can create complacency. The lifestyle may include small luxuries, predictable routines, and a feeling of safety, but it rarely leads to significant wealth.

Comfort is seductive because it feels like success compared to what came before. Yet it can also become a trap. As income rises, so does lifestyle inflation. Instead of investing the extra margin, many spend it on upgrades — nicer homes, cars, and vacations — believing this is the reward for their hard work. The problem is that comfort players rarely prioritize building scalable income or assets. They focus on maintaining their lifestyle rather than positioning themselves for exponential growth.

The Growth Game

The third game is growth. People in this stage have shifted their focus from immediate comfort to long-term wealth. They begin investing in skills, building assets, and seeking opportunities that create leverage. Growth players measure success not by what they earn today but by the systems and structures they are creating for the future.

This game requires a significant mindset shift. Growth players are willing to delay gratification, reinvesting profits instead of spending them. They study opportunities others overlook, such as scalable businesses, high-value skill sets, or investments that compound over decades. While their lifestyle may not appear flashy, their wealth grows quietly in the background. This is where most self-made millionaires operate, often unnoticed by those still chasing visible signs of success.

The final stage is what can be called the freedom game. This is where money stops being a constant concern and becomes a tool for designing life on your own terms. Freedom players are not motivated by accumulating possessions or proving success to others. Their focus is autonomy — the ability to choose how they spend their time, where they live, and what they pursue without financial constraints dictating those choices.

Reaching this stage requires a very different mindset than the earlier games. While growth focuses on building and expanding, freedom focuses on simplification and alignment. Wealth becomes less about chasing more and more about securing what truly matters. For some, that might mean continuing to grow their businesses or investments. For others, it means maintaining a level of financial independence that supports meaningful work, travel, or family life. The defining trait is control. Freedom players do not feel trapped by obligations, and they have systems in place that allow their wealth to sustain itself.

Transitions between these games are rarely linear. People can slip backward if they are not careful, especially during major life changes like job loss, family obligations, or economic downturns. This is why understanding the game you are playing is so crucial. Without clarity, it is easy to mistake comfort for security or confuse visible success with true freedom. Many who appear wealthy are still operating within the comfort game, tied to high expenses and constant work, while others with modest lifestyles quietly play at the freedom level.

Moving from one game to the next requires intentional shifts. Escaping survival demands learning how to manage limited resources and begin building even a small margin for investment. Leaving comfort behind requires resisting lifestyle creep and redirecting surplus toward assets rather than consumption. Entering growth calls for embracing delayed gratification and prioritizing systems over short-term wins. Finally, stepping into freedom means rethinking what "enough" looks like and designing life around values rather than endless accumulation.

One of the most powerful insights is that the rules for each game are different. Strategies that work in survival — like cutting costs and focusing on stability — may hold you back in growth, where taking calculated risks becomes necessary. Habits that build growth — constant reinvestment and expansion — may not serve you in freedom, where preserving and simplifying can create more fulfillment than relentless scaling. Recognizing these shifts allows you to play the right strategy at the right time rather than clinging to outdated approaches.

Understanding these four games also reframes how you view others. Instead of comparing lifestyles or feeling behind, you start to see where people are positioned and what strategies they are using. This clarity removes much of the anxiety that comes from social comparison and replaces it with focus on your own trajectory. The goal is not to copy anyone else's path but to identify the game you are currently in and determine what actions will move you closer to the one you want to play next.

This awareness becomes the foundation for everything that follows. When you know the game, you can finally stop playing by someone else's rules and begin building a strategy that works for you. The chapters ahead will deepen this understanding, showing how to create leverage, build skills, and design systems that allow you to progress steadily from survival to freedom without falling into the traps that keep most people circling the same levels for years.

The Wealth Ladders

Building wealth is often described as a climb, but most people imagine it as a single ladder: work hard, earn more, save diligently, and eventually reach financial security. In reality, there are multiple ladders, each representing a different level of financial thinking and strategy. Knowing which ladder you are on — and which you need to climb next — is crucial, because the skills and choices that help you rise on one ladder will not necessarily carry you higher on another.

The First Ladder: Earning to Survive

The first wealth ladder is about survival. People at this level earn just enough to cover basic needs — food, rent, transportation, and other essentials. The focus is on income stability rather than growth. Every paycheck is already spoken for, and financial emergencies can easily cause setbacks. While there is honor in working hard to meet immediate needs, staying on this ladder too long creates chronic stress and leaves no room for future planning.

Progress from this level begins when someone moves beyond reactive living and creates even a small buffer. That buffer might come from reducing unnecessary expenses, finding additional income streams, or learning new skills that lead to higher pay. The critical shift here is moving from thinking only about "getting by" to asking, "How can I create breathing room?" This small gap becomes the seed for future growth.

The Second Ladder: Earning for Comfort

Once basic needs are met, most people climb to the comfort ladder. Here, income exceeds expenses enough to allow small luxuries — a nicer apartment, regular dining out, vacations, or personal hobbies. Life feels easier and more enjoyable, and the constant stress of survival begins to fade. For many, this stage feels like success, especially compared to where they started.

The danger of the comfort ladder is complacency. Extra income often fuels lifestyle upgrades instead of wealth-building. People begin to measure progress by visible markers — a better car, a bigger home, more frequent travel — rather than by assets or freedom. This keeps them tied to their income, even if they are technically earning more than ever. The comfort ladder can feel like a reward, but it is also a trap if you are not careful.

Without deliberate planning, people can spend decades here without ever moving closer to true financial independence.

The Third Ladder: Earning to Grow

The growth ladder begins when someone realizes that extra income is not enough. What matters is how that income is used. At this stage, people start prioritizing investments, skill-building, and systems that create long-term value. Instead of asking, "How can I earn more?" they begin asking, "How can I make what I earn work for me?" This shift from active income to leveraged income is the foundation of quiet wealth.

Growth at this level often requires uncomfortable decisions. It may mean resisting lifestyle inflation to funnel resources into investments. It may involve taking calculated risks, like launching a side business, buying assets, or developing expertise that positions you for higher-value opportunities. The focus is no longer just on stability or comfort but on creating momentum that compounds over time.

The highest ladder is freedom. This stage is reached when wealth is no longer about accumulation but about autonomy. Money becomes a tool, not the central focus of life. Instead of chasing more for the sake of more, people on this ladder design their finances to support what truly matters to them — whether that is creative work, family, travel, or simply the ability to choose their own pace of living. Freedom is not defined by a specific number in the bank but by the level of independence that number provides. Reaching this stage requires more than just having enough money. It demands a shift in identity. Many who arrive at financial independence struggle because they have been conditioned to equate worth with productivity. Without the constant pressure to earn, they can feel untethered. Those who thrive at this level recognize that freedom is as much about purpose as it is about wealth. They redirect energy toward meaningful pursuits rather than falling into the trap of endlessly scaling for no reason other than habit.

Moving between ladders is rarely smooth. People can rise and fall depending on life circumstances, market changes, or personal choices. Someone may reach growth but slip back into comfort if they begin spending aggressively after a raise. Another person might leap ahead to freedom by selling a business or receiving a windfall, only to find themselves unprepared to manage it. Understanding that these ladders are dynamic helps you approach them with humility and adaptability rather than frustration when progress feels uneven.

A critical insight is that the strategies for each ladder are not interchangeable. What works for survival — strict budgeting and maximizing every paycheck — can hold you back in growth, where risk and reinvestment become essential. Likewise, habits that drive growth — relentless expansion, constant scaling — can undermine freedom if they prevent you from ever stepping off the treadmill. The key is to recognize when it is time to evolve your approach rather than clinging to the tactics that worked in a previous stage.

Climbing the wealth ladders is not just about financial tactics but about awareness. It requires asking where you truly are, not where you wish you were. Are you still reacting to emergencies, or have you begun to think about leverage and assets? Are you prioritizing visible comfort over long-term security? Have you defined what freedom looks like for you, or are you chasing an endless finish line set by others? Honest answers to these questions reveal not only your current position but also the next step required to move forward.

The purpose of understanding these ladders is not to rush through them as fast as possible but to navigate them intentionally. Each level teaches valuable lessons — discipline in survival, gratitude in comfort, vision in growth, and alignment in freedom. When approached deliberately, the climb becomes less about escaping one stage and more about mastering it on the way to the next. This awareness prepares you for the deeper principles that follow, where mindset and action combine to accelerate your progress toward a life designed on your own terms.

Decoding Leverage and Multiplication

Wealth does not grow by working harder alone. It grows when effort, capital, and time are multiplied through leverage. Leverage is the quiet force behind most significant fortunes. It allows one action to produce results far greater than what the same action would yield on its own. Understanding how to use leverage is what separates those who remain dependent on constant labor from those who quietly create freedom.

What Leverage Really Means

Leverage is often misunderstood. Many people think of it only in terms of financial borrowing, like using debt to buy property or invest in a business. While financial leverage is one form, it is only one piece of the picture. True leverage can take many shapes: skills, technology, systems, and relationships can all multiply results without requiring proportional increases in effort.

Consider a skilled professional who learns how to document their expertise in a course or book. Instead of trading time for each client, they create something once and sell it repeatedly. The same knowledge that once served one person at a time now reaches hundreds or thousands. This is multiplication at work: the same effort creates exponentially larger impact and returns.

The Difference Between Addition and Multiplication

Most people approach money with an additive mindset. They think in terms of incremental progress: a raise here, a side job there, saving a little more each month. While addition can improve circumstances, it rarely leads to freedom. Multiplication, on the other hand, changes the scale of what is possible. When you apply multiplication, one decision — acquiring a skill, building a system, investing in the right asset — creates outcomes that continue to grow even when you are not actively involved.

This shift requires rethinking how you spend time and energy. Instead of asking, "How can I do more?" the better question becomes, "How can I create something that continues to work without me?" This is why entrepreneurs, investors, and creators often accelerate faster than those who rely solely on employment income. Their efforts compound because they have built vehicles that generate value repeatedly without requiring constant input.

Leverage in Everyday Life

You do not need massive capital or advanced technical knowledge to begin using leverage. Many forms of leverage are accessible right now. Automation tools, for example, allow you to manage tasks that once required hours of manual effort. Networking with the right people can open opportunities that no amount of solitary grinding could unlock. Even habits can serve as leverage: the discipline of consistently investing or creating builds momentum that compounds over years.

The first step is identifying where your current approach relies entirely on your direct effort. If every dollar you earn depends on your presence and time, you are limited by your own capacity. Leverage begins when you find ways to separate income from constant activity, even in small ways at first. This might mean creating repeatable systems in your work, learning a skill that scales in value, or channeling resources into assets that grow without your ongoing labor.

One of the most powerful forms of leverage is financial. This includes investments, compounding returns, and the strategic use of borrowed capital. When managed carefully, financial leverage allows resources to grow far faster than what regular saving could achieve. For example, money placed into appreciating assets such as index funds, real estate, or well-vetted business ventures compounds year after year, quietly building momentum in the background. The key is understanding the difference between productive debt and destructive debt — borrowing to acquire assets that generate income is fundamentally different from borrowing to fund consumption that loses value over time.

Skill-based leverage is equally important. High-value skills are assets that do not depreciate and often create exponential opportunities. A person who understands marketing, coding, or financial analysis can apply those abilities in multiple contexts, whether launching a business, consulting, or building scalable products. The return on skill leverage is not only financial but also positional; the more unique your expertise, the more control you have over opportunities and negotiations. This is why the quiet wealthy often invest heavily in continuous learning, stacking complementary skills to create combinations few others can replicate.

Networks provide another dimension of multiplication. Connections with the right people can open doors that would otherwise remain closed. A single introduction can lead to partnerships, clients, or investments that accelerate growth far beyond what you could achieve alone. Networks also provide leverage by pooling resources — knowledge, capital, influence — that magnify the impact of individual actions. Building authentic relationships rather than transactional ones is what turns networks into lasting leverage.

Technology has become an unprecedented force multiplier in modern wealth creation. Tools that automate processes, amplify communication, and reduce friction allow individuals to achieve results that once required entire teams. A single person can now reach millions through content, run businesses with minimal overhead, and manage investments with tools that were previously available only to institutions. Embracing technology as leverage means constantly asking how to make systems work on your behalf rather than doing everything manually.

Combining these forms of leverage is where true multiplication occurs. Financial resources invested into technology or skill development create compounding advantages. A strong network can accelerate the results of both capital and expertise. When multiple forms of leverage intersect, growth is no longer linear; small actions taken at the right time ripple outward, creating impact far greater than the initial effort.

The challenge for most people is recognizing that leverage often feels counterintuitive. It requires stepping away from constant busyness and toward designing systems that operate without direct input. This can feel uncomfortable for those raised to equate work with worth. Yet once you experience the effects of leverage — income arriving while you sleep, opportunities appearing because of previous investments in skills or relationships — it becomes impossible to return to a purely linear model of effort.

Mastering leverage and multiplication is not about shortcuts or avoiding effort altogether. It is about directing energy into areas where the return is amplified rather than diminished. This mindset shift turns ordinary actions into seeds for extraordinary outcomes. As you apply these principles, you begin to see wealth not as a reward for endless work but as the natural result of aligning your efforts with forces that multiply rather than merely add.

Part II. Rewiring Your Financial Mindset

The biggest shift on your journey to building lasting wealth will not come from a single strategy or investment. It will come from changing the way you think about money at its core. Most people believe wealth begins with action — a side hustle, a better job, a savings plan — but every decision you make about money originates from the beliefs you carry about what is possible, what you deserve, and how the game of wealth is played. If those beliefs remain unexamined, even the best tactics will eventually fall apart.

This part of the book is about uncovering and replacing the mental scripts that quietly shape your financial life. These scripts are rarely chosen; they are absorbed over years from family, culture, and personal experiences. Some are rooted in fear, like believing that there will never be enough. Others seem positive on the surface, such as equating hard work with guaranteed success, yet still limit your ability to see opportunities outside familiar patterns. Left unchallenged, these beliefs can keep you locked in cycles of earning and spending that feel responsible but never create true freedom.

Rewiring your mindset does not mean ignoring practical action. It means aligning your thoughts and habits so they work in the same direction rather than against each other. When your beliefs about money are outdated or conflicting, progress feels like pushing uphill — each gain is quickly undone by unconscious behaviors. When you shift those beliefs, the uphill climb flattens. Decisions that once felt stressful become natural. Opportunities that seemed invisible start to appear. The path to growth becomes clearer because you are no longer sabotaging it with hidden assumptions.

This section will guide you through that process step by step. You will identify the scarcity scripts you inherited, learn how to rewrite them, and begin constructing a mindset rooted in abundance and value creation. Rather than simply telling you to "think positive," these chapters will show you how to replace vague optimism with grounded confidence —

confidence built on understanding how money actually works and how to position yourself within that reality.

By the end of this part, you will have more than new insights. You will have a new operating system for every financial choice you make. This mindset will set the stage for the actions that follow, allowing you to move into wealth-building strategies with clarity, focus, and a level of conviction that most people never reach.

Chapter 3: The Psychology of Scarcity vs. Abundance

The Scarcity Scripts You Inherited

Every belief you hold about money has an origin. The way you react to opportunities, the decisions you make about saving or spending, and even the risks you are willing to take are all influenced by scripts you absorbed long before you were conscious of them. These scripts, often passed down from family, culture, or early life experiences, form the invisible framework behind your financial behavior. Many of them are rooted in scarcity — the assumption that there is never enough and that life is a zero-sum game where someone else's gain must come at your loss.

How Scarcity Scripts Are Formed

Scarcity scripts often begin in childhood. If you grew up hearing phrases like "we can't afford that," "money doesn't grow on trees," or "rich people are greedy," those messages left an imprint. Even if your circumstances have changed, the beliefs remain. Psychologist Brad Klontz, who studied financial behaviors extensively, found that these early "money scripts" operate unconsciously and often drive financial decisions well into adulthood. A person raised with scarcity messages may avoid investing, underprice their skills, or overvalue security to the point of missing opportunities.

Cultural narratives amplify these scripts. Many societies glorify self-sacrifice and frugality, equating them with morality, while subtly framing wealth as suspect or undeserved. This dual message — work hard but never aspire too high — creates internal conflict. You may want more for yourself but feel guilty for desiring it, as if ambition is selfish. Over time, this conflict becomes a quiet barrier to action, keeping you from pursuing opportunities that could dramatically change your financial trajectory.

The Hidden Costs of Scarcity Thinking

Scarcity does not just affect how much you earn; it shapes how you think. When you believe resources are limited, your focus narrows to immediate needs and short-term survival. This is why people caught in financial stress often struggle to plan for the future — their mental bandwidth is consumed by the next bill, the next paycheck, the next problem. Research by Sendhil Mullainathan and Eldar Shafir has shown that scarcity impairs decision-making, reducing cognitive capacity and leading to choices that unintentionally reinforce the very conditions people are trying to escape.

This mindset also affects risk tolerance. Scarcity teaches you to avoid loss at all costs, which often means avoiding opportunity as well. The fear of making a wrong move can paralyze you into making no move at all. Ironically, this caution can keep you stuck in the very situations you are trying to rise above. The wealthy play by different rules not because they are reckless, but because they understand that controlled risk is necessary for growth.

Recognizing the Scripts in Your Own Life

The first step in rewriting these scripts is identifying them. Scarcity beliefs often hide in plain sight, disguised as "common sense" or "being realistic." They surface in subtle ways: hesitation to invest even when you have the means, guilt over wanting a better lifestyle, or an automatic assumption that opportunities are "for other people." These thoughts may feel natural because you have carried them for so long, but they are learned patterns, not universal truths.

Start by paying attention to your internal dialogue about money. Do you default to fear when thinking about expenses or opportunities? Do you find yourself clinging to security even when it limits growth? Becoming aware of these patterns is not about blaming your upbringing or culture; it is about understanding the lens through which you currently see money so you can begin to change it.

Rewriting scarcity scripts begins with consciously challenging the assumptions that shaped them. It requires asking where each belief came from and whether it still serves you. A message that may have been protective in the past, like "save every penny because life is uncertain," can turn into a barrier when you need to invest in opportunities that create growth. By examining the origin of these beliefs, you begin to separate what was circumstantial from what is actually true for your current reality.

This process is not about rejecting everything you were taught but about filtering it. Some lessons about responsibility and prudence remain valuable, while others must be updated to align with your goals. The shift is subtle yet profound: moving from "I can't" to "how can I?" transforms the way you evaluate options. Suddenly, possibilities that once felt out of reach become solvable problems rather than permanent barriers.

Replacing scarcity with abundance does not mean reckless optimism. It means adopting a mindset that assumes value can be created and expanded rather than hoarded. This perspective encourages curiosity and problem-solving. Instead of focusing on what you lack, you begin asking what skills, relationships, or strategies you can build to generate more. Over time, this reorientation changes the quality of your decisions. You move from reactive choices driven by fear to proactive strategies grounded in confidence.

Practical steps reinforce this mental shift. Exposure to new ideas and people is one of the most powerful. When you spend time around individuals who approach money from a place of growth rather than fear, your own thinking begins to expand. Their habits — investing early, taking calculated risks, seeking leverage — challenge old assumptions and normalize behaviors that once felt foreign. This is why environment matters so deeply; beliefs are contagious, and surrounding yourself with the right influences accelerates change.

Another step is tracking evidence of progress. Scarcity thinking thrives on the narrative that nothing is ever enough, which can blind you to the improvements you are making. Documenting milestones, even small ones, trains your brain to notice growth rather than lack. This builds confidence and creates momentum, making it easier to sustain new habits that replace old patterns.

Dismantling scarcity scripts also involves developing patience. Shifting from survival-oriented thinking to abundance takes time, especially if those beliefs have been reinforced for years. You may find yourself slipping back into old fears during moments of stress or uncertainty. The key is not perfection but persistence — recognizing the slip, reframing the thought, and continuing forward without judgment. Over time, the new patterns begin to feel natural, and scarcity loses its hold.

The most profound change occurs when you internalize the idea that wealth is not fixed but created. The resources you seek are not limited to what currently exists; they expand through innovation, service, and the ability to solve problems for others. This realization removes the sense of competition that scarcity fosters and replaces it with collaboration and creativity. It shifts your focus from fighting for a slice of a limited pie to learning how to bake a bigger one.

When these new scripts take hold, everything else you do with money — from earning and investing to saving and spending — starts to feel different. Decisions that once triggered fear become opportunities for growth. You stop asking whether you deserve wealth and start focusing on how to build and steward it responsibly. This mindset becomes the foundation for the practical strategies ahead, ensuring that every action you take is supported rather than sabotaged by the beliefs driving it.

Reprogramming Your Money Identity

Your relationship with money is not just about what you do; it is about who you believe you are. Beneath every financial habit — whether saving diligently, overspending impulsively, or hesitating to invest — lies an identity you have formed around money. This identity quietly answers questions you may never consciously ask: Do I see myself as someone who deserves wealth? Do I believe I am capable of managing it? Do I feel comfortable with abundance, or do I secretly expect it to disappear?

These internal definitions are rarely examined, yet they shape every choice you make. If you believe you are "bad with money," you will unconsciously reinforce that belief by avoiding opportunities to learn or grow. If you see wealth as something "other people" achieve, you will filter yourself out of possibilities that could lead there. Reprogramming your money identity means rewriting these internal definitions so they align with the person you want to become, not the limitations you have carried until now.

The Origin of Money Identity

Money identity is built over time through experience and repetition. The messages you heard growing up — about work, wealth, and what is "normal" for people like you — create a baseline expectation. Perhaps you were taught that financial success requires extreme sacrifice, or that wealth comes only to the lucky. These early impressions become mental shortcuts that guide behavior long after circumstances have changed.

Personal experiences reinforce these beliefs. A failed business venture, a period of debt, or a financial windfall can all leave emotional imprints. Without awareness, you may internalize these events as reflections of who you are rather than what happened. Someone who lost money once might unconsciously avoid risk forever, while someone who experienced a sudden gain might fear losing it and spend recklessly as a result.

Why Identity Shapes Behavior More Than Willpower

Many people try to improve their finances by focusing on tactics: budgeting, saving, or finding ways to earn more. While these strategies matter, they often fail when they conflict with underlying identity. A person who sees themselves as "always broke" may sabotage progress because success feels unfamiliar. This is why willpower alone is rarely enough to sustain lasting change. Identity acts like an internal thermostat, pulling you back toward what feels normal, even if normal is not what you want.

To create lasting transformation, you must raise that internal thermostat. This is not about pretending you are wealthy when you are not. It is about aligning your self-concept with growth rather than limitation. When you see yourself as someone who creates value, manages resources wisely, and deserves abundance, your decisions naturally begin to reflect that belief. Habits follow identity, not the other way around.

The Power of Conscious Reprogramming

Reprogramming your money identity begins with awareness, but it deepens through intentional practice. Each time you make a decision that contradicts an old belief — negotiating a raise when you once felt unworthy, investing in learning when you once hesitated to spend — you reinforce a new identity. Over time, these actions accumulate, building a sense of congruence between who you believe you are and how you behave with money.

One of the most effective ways to shift your money identity is to deliberately expose yourself to new financial experiences that challenge old narratives. This does not have to mean massive risks or unrealistic leaps. It can be as simple as making decisions that reflect trust in your ability to grow — investing in a course to learn a skill you once doubted you could master, setting aside money to build an emergency fund when saving used to feel impossible, or intentionally choosing to view money as a tool rather than a source of stress. Each of these actions sends a signal to your subconscious that you are no longer living under the same limitations.

Anchoring your new identity requires consistency. It is not enough to declare, "I am good with money" and expect transformation to follow. You must back it up with repeated proof. Tracking your wins, no matter how small, helps solidify this shift. A month of staying on budget, negotiating a small increase in income, or consistently contributing to savings all reinforce that you are someone who follows through and creates results. The more evidence you accumulate, the stronger your belief becomes.

Language plays a powerful role in this process. The words you use to describe yourself shape how you see yourself. Pay attention to casual phrases like "I'm terrible with numbers" or "I'll never be rich" — they are more than throwaway comments. They are instructions to your brain, constantly reinforcing an identity you are trying to outgrow. Replace them with language that reflects growth: "I am learning to manage my money well," or "I am building skills that increase my earning power." These statements do not deny your current reality; they affirm the direction you are choosing to move in.

Environment also influences identity. Surrounding yourself with people and information that normalize growth can accelerate the shift. If your current circle constantly reinforces scarcity or fear, you will unconsciously adopt the same attitudes. Seeking out communities — online or in person — where financial growth is discussed openly and realistically helps you see what is possible and reduces the sense that abundance is only for others. Over time, the behaviors and beliefs of that environment become part of your own.

This reprogramming process is not about perfection. Old scripts will resurface, especially during moments of stress or uncertainty. The difference is that you will recognize them and choose not to follow them. Each time you notice an outdated belief and replace it with a new response, you weaken its hold and strengthen your new identity. Gradually, the thoughts and behaviors that once felt forced become automatic. You begin to act from a place of quiet confidence rather than fear or doubt.

Ultimately, reprogramming your money identity allows you to make financial decisions that align with the future you are creating rather than the past you inherited. It closes the gap between what you desire and what you believe is possible. When your self-concept shifts, strategies that once seemed overwhelming become manageable. The opportunities you once overlooked start to feel attainable. This internal alignment becomes the foundation for lasting change, setting you up for every action you will take in the chapters ahead.

The Abundance Operating System

Shifting from scarcity to abundance is more than just adopting a positive outlook. It is about building a new internal framework that influences every financial choice you make. This framework, an "operating system," is what determines whether you default to fear and limitation or move toward creativity and growth. When you begin to view money and opportunity as expansive rather than finite, you stop competing for scraps and start creating value that benefits both yourself and others.

Why an Operating System Matters

An operating system is the underlying code that runs everything else. Just as a phone's software dictates how its apps function, your internal money operating system dictates how your strategies perform. You can try new budgets, investments, or side hustles, but if your internal programming still expects struggle, those strategies will eventually break down. Abundance rewiring addresses the root issue, ensuring that every tactic you adopt builds on a foundation of possibility rather than fear.

Most people do not realize they are running on outdated code. Scarcity programming is passed down subtly through family beliefs, cultural norms, and personal experiences. It shows up in thoughts like "money is hard to come by," "wealth makes people greedy," or "there is never enough to go around." These beliefs may have originated as protective mechanisms — especially if your family faced hardship — but they no longer serve you in an environment where opportunities can be created rather than merely found.

Core Principles of Abundance

At its core, the abundance operating system rests on three principles: value is created, growth is possible, and opportunities are renewable. Value is created means wealth is not a fixed pie. Instead of fighting for a slice, you can build something new that adds value to others and in turn rewards you. Growth is possible acknowledges that skills, income, and opportunities can all be developed rather than being fixed traits. Opportunities are renewable reframes failure, reminding you that losing one chance does not mean there will never be another.

These principles fundamentally change how you approach decisions. In scarcity, every mistake feels catastrophic. In abundance, mistakes are feedback that guides your next attempt. Scarcity encourages hoarding and hesitation. Abundance encourages calculated action and reinvestment. Over time, these patterns compound, creating a gap between those who stay stuck and those who steadily build quiet wealth.

Recognizing the Triggers

Before you can fully install a new operating system, you must identify the triggers that activate your old one. Notice when fear drives your decisions — whether that is panic over spending money, reluctance to invest in yourself, or a tendency to fixate on what you lack. These moments reveal where old programming still lingers. Awareness alone does not fix them, but it allows you to pause, question, and choose differently rather than acting automatically.

This process also involves paying attention to language. Words like "never," "always," or "impossible" often signal scarcity thinking. When you catch yourself saying, "I'll never get ahead," or "It's impossible to earn that much," pause and reframe the statement. Ask what would have to change for it to be possible. This shift from resignation to curiosity opens doors you could not see before.

Installing a new operating system for abundance happens through repeated practice, not a single breakthrough moment. The shift solidifies when you consistently make choices aligned with growth rather than fear. One of the most effective ways to begin is by reframing how you view money itself. Instead of treating it as something scarce to be hoarded, see it as a resource that flows through your life. This perspective encourages circulation — earning, saving, investing, and spending intentionally — rather than clinging to every dollar out of anxiety.

Small daily actions create the foundation for this mindset. Choosing to invest in learning a new skill rather than avoiding the expense, saving consistently even when the amount feels insignificant, or setting aside time to evaluate opportunities rather than rushing into them are all ways of signaling to yourself that you operate from possibility. These decisions compound, gradually building evidence that you are capable of growth and worthy of it.

Visualization can reinforce this shift. When you picture yourself handling greater financial responsibility with calm and clarity, you train your mind to normalize that identity. This does not mean pretending you already have what you want; it means preparing yourself mentally for the person you are becoming. When opportunities arise, you are less likely to self-sabotage because they feel congruent with the image you have been rehearsing internally.

Environment plays a pivotal role as well. Surrounding yourself with information and people that reflect abundance keeps you from slipping back into scarcity thinking. If every conversation you have reinforces fear about the economy, layoffs, or debt, it will be difficult to think expansively. Curate your inputs — books, podcasts, mentors, peers — so they remind you of possibility and solutions rather than limitations. Over time, this new input rewires your default responses, much like updating the software of a device.

Tracking progress is another practical layer of the abundance operating system. Scarcity focuses on what is missing; abundance recognizes growth. By documenting milestones, no matter how small, you train your brain to see evidence that things are moving forward. This practice builds patience, which is essential for compounding results. Instead of seeking immediate transformation, you learn to trust that small improvements over time lead to profound change.

The final piece is aligning your actions with the values you want your wealth to reflect. Abundance is not simply about having more; it is about creating enough to live meaningfully and contribute to others. When your financial growth is tied to purpose — providing for family, building something valuable, creating opportunities — it becomes self-reinforcing. Each step forward affirms not only what you are achieving but also why it matters.

Over time, this new operating system becomes the default. Situations that once triggered fear now prompt curiosity. Decisions that used to feel risky begin to feel strategic. You no longer measure success solely by income or possessions but by freedom, alignment, and the ability to create impact. This is where wealth stops being a distant dream and becomes an integrated part of who you are, guiding every choice you make from a place of quiet confidence and possibility.

Chapter 4: Value Creation as the Core of Wealth

Why Value > Effort > Time

Most people are taught to see money as a direct trade for time. The logic is simple: work a certain number of hours, receive a certain amount of pay. This belief is reinforced early in life and continues through school and traditional employment. The harder you work and the more hours you put in, the more you should earn — at least in theory. But if this were true, the hardest-working people in the world would be the wealthiest, and that is rarely the case.

The real driver of wealth is not time, nor even raw effort, but the value you bring to the marketplace. Value is what determines why one person earns ten times more than another for seemingly less effort or fewer hours. It explains why certain skills command premium pay and why some opportunities scale exponentially while others plateau no matter how hard you work. Understanding this hierarchy — value over effort over time — is the key to breaking free from income ceilings and building lasting financial freedom.

Time as the Lowest Form of Currency

Time is finite. No matter how skilled or motivated you are, there are only so many hours in a day. When your income is tied directly to time, you face an inherent limit. This is why hourly wages and salaried positions, while stable, rarely lead to extraordinary wealth. Even high-paying professions can become a trap if earnings depend entirely on personal output. Doctors, lawyers, and consultants can find themselves exhausted, trading long hours for high income but with little room to scale.

This time-for-money trade creates a subtle psychological barrier as well. It conditions you to equate more hours with more success, reinforcing hustle culture and burnout. The idea of stepping back or delegating feels dangerous because income appears to vanish the moment you stop working. Breaking this mindset requires recognizing that time should not be your primary currency — value should.

Effort Without Value Still Limits You

Effort often feels like progress because it is visible. Working harder, staying late, or pushing through weekends gives a sense of control and accomplishment. But effort alone does not guarantee higher income or impact. Many people exert extraordinary energy in roles that generate little value, resulting in frustration and stagnation. They may be praised for their dedication yet remain stuck at the same financial level because the marketplace rewards outcomes, not sweat.

The truth is that effort must be directed toward creating value for others. Value is what someone is willing to pay for, not the hours you logged to deliver it. This is why two people can work equally hard — or even with similar skills — and achieve vastly different results. One has learned to align effort with high-value outcomes; the other pours energy into tasks that do not scale or matter to the people they serve.

Value as the Multiplier

Value operates differently than time or effort. It is not inherently capped and can scale far beyond personal limits. When you create something people deeply need or desire — a product, a service, an idea, or even specialized knowledge — the marketplace rewards you in proportion to its impact. This is why creators, entrepreneurs, and investors often build wealth that far exceeds what traditional employment could ever provide. Their focus is not on how many hours they work but on how much value their work generates. The hierarchy becomes clear: time matters least, effort matters more, and value matters most. The challenge is learning how to shift from measuring success by hours or activity to measuring it by the value you create.

Increasing the value you create begins with understanding what people truly need and are willing to pay for. This requires shifting your focus outward. Instead of asking, "How can I earn more?" the better question is, "What problem can I solve that others consider highly valuable?" Value is determined by impact, not by how much effort you put in. A single insight that saves a business thousands of dollars is worth far more than days of unfocused labor.

One practical way to increase value is to deepen your expertise in areas where demand is high and supply is limited. Specialized knowledge almost always commands higher rewards than generalized effort. A person who understands a rare technology, negotiates complex deals, or communicates solutions in a way others cannot will naturally stand out in the marketplace. The same is true for combining skills in unique ways — pairing marketing knowledge with design or financial expertise with storytelling creates intersections where few competitors exist. This stacking of abilities often multiplies value far beyond what any single skill could achieve on its own.

Another lever is scalability. When the outcome of your work can reach many people at once rather than serving only one person at a time, value multiplies without proportional increases in effort. A teacher who tutors one student earns only for those hours, but a teacher who builds an online course reaches thousands while doing the work once. Similarly, an investor who places capital in the right opportunities benefits from returns that grow even while they focus elsewhere. Multiplication happens whenever the result of your effort can keep producing without constant personal input.

A crucial part of this shift is detaching your sense of worth from constant activity. Many people feel guilty stepping back from endless work because they have equated busyness with success. True leverage comes when you are comfortable allowing systems, tools, or people to extend your impact while you focus on higher-level decisions. This is not avoidance of work but an evolution of it. By stepping out of purely executional roles and into roles where you design, direct, and refine, you create room for exponential growth.

It is also important to measure progress differently. Instead of tracking hours or even tasks completed, begin evaluating outcomes. Did this project move you closer to your long-term goals? Did it create enduring impact for others? This mindset shift frees you from the cycle of endless hustle and encourages you to focus on results that compound over time. It also naturally improves decision-making, since you begin prioritizing opportunities that offer the highest return on value rather than simply the highest immediate paycheck.

Ultimately, the principle of value over effort and time changes how you approach your career, your business, and your financial strategies. It encourages you to invest energy where it will have the greatest multiplier effect and to stop equating harder work with better results. Once this becomes part of your thinking, opportunities that once felt out of reach start to appear within grasp. You begin building wealth not by doing more of the same but by elevating the level of value you provide — and that shift, more than any single tactic, is what creates freedom that lasts.

Finding the Problems Worth Solving

Every opportunity to create wealth is tied to a problem waiting to be solved. The bigger and more urgent the problem, the greater the value in solving it. Yet most people never stop to ask which problems are truly worth their time. They focus on minor inconveniences or low-value tasks, pouring in energy that leads to limited rewards. To build lasting financial freedom, you must learn to identify problems with high impact — problems that matter deeply to others and create meaningful transformation when resolved.

Understanding Value Through Problems

Value is a reflection of need. When someone pays for a product or service, they are not buying the thing itself but the relief it provides. A medication is not about the pill; it is about ending pain. A financial service is not about spreadsheets; it is about peace of mind and security. The more pressing the need, the more people are willing to invest in a solution.

This perspective shifts how you approach opportunities. Instead of asking, "What can I sell?" or "What skill do I have?" begin with, "What pain point is big enough that someone will pay to have it solved?" People rarely spend on minor discomforts, but they will pay generously to remove something that feels urgent, costly, or emotionally heavy.

The Three Layers of Problems

Problems can be categorized by depth. The first layer is surface-level inconvenience. These are annoyances people wish were better but can live with — like slow customer service or minor tech glitches. Solving these often leads to modest rewards because the pain is not intense enough to demand urgent action.

The second layer is practical pain. These problems interfere with goals or create clear obstacles, such as inefficiencies costing a company thousands of dollars or health habits leading to chronic fatigue. Solutions here tend to command higher value because the impact is measurable and tangible.

The deepest layer is identity-level pain. These problems touch people's sense of self or future. Financial insecurity, loss of confidence, or fear of missing out on life opportunities fall into this category. When a solution addresses this level, it creates transformation rather than convenience — and transformation is where the highest value lies.

Spotting High-Value Problems

High-value problems share several characteristics. They are widely felt, emotionally charged, and carry real consequences if left unsolved. They may involve financial costs, wasted time, missed opportunities, or emotional stress. The best opportunities often sit where personal frustration intersects with broader demand. If you find yourself thinking, "Why hasn't anyone fixed this yet?" and discover many others share that sentiment, you have likely uncovered a valuable problem.

To spot these opportunities, observe carefully. Listen to complaints, watch where people spend disproportionate time or money, and notice recurring frustrations. Market research can help, but so can simply paying attention in everyday life. Patterns emerge in conversations, reviews, and even your own experiences. The problems worth solving rarely hide; they are in plain sight for those willing to look closely.

Evaluating which problems are worth solving starts with considering your unique position. Not every high-value problem will be right for you. Some require resources or expertise you do not yet have, while others may not align with your values or long-term vision. The sweet spot lies where significant need meets your ability to contribute something distinct. When your skills, experiences, and insights allow you to solve a pressing issue in a way others cannot, you create leverage that goes far beyond competing on effort alone.

A practical way to assess this is by asking three key questions. First, is this problem painful enough that people are actively seeking solutions? If potential customers are already spending time or money trying to fix it, that is a clear indicator of value. Second, is the pain urgent? People prioritize solutions that feel immediate rather than abstract or distant. Third, does solving this problem align with your strengths or an area you are willing to grow into? The closer the alignment, the more likely you are to create a solution that feels authentic and sustainable.

Testing the value of a problem before committing fully is critical. Too many people pour months or years into building solutions without confirming that anyone actually wants them. Early validation can be as simple as conversations with potential customers, small experiments, or low-cost prototypes. The goal is to gather evidence that the problem is real, that your solution resonates, and that people are willing to pay for it. This step reduces risk and helps you refine your approach before scaling.

Once you confirm a problem is worth solving, the focus shifts to positioning your solution effectively. High-value problems often attract competition, and differentiation becomes essential. Instead of aiming to be slightly better, aim to be meaningfully different. That difference might come from speed, personalization, depth of service, or a unique combination of skills you bring to the table. The clearer and more specific your positioning, the easier it becomes to stand out and communicate why your approach matters.

As you develop solutions, it is equally important to think about scalability. A problem may be valuable to solve for one person, but its real potential emerges when you can serve many without proportionally increasing your effort. This might involve creating systems, leveraging technology, or packaging your knowledge into repeatable formats. Solving problems at scale is where value multiplies and where sustainable wealth begins to form.

Finally, the problems worth solving are rarely static. Markets evolve, technology advances, and new challenges emerge. Maintaining a mindset of curiosity ensures you stay alert to shifts and can pivot when necessary. The ability to adapt — to see where unmet needs are moving and reposition yourself ahead of them — is what separates those who briefly capitalize on an opportunity from those who build enduring success.

When you learn to identify and evaluate the right problems, you stop chasing random opportunities and start focusing on the ones that truly matter. These are the problems that transform lives when solved — including your own — and they form the foundation for every meaningful wealth-building strategy you will explore in the chapters that follow.

Packaging Value for Maximum Impact

Creating value is only the first step toward building wealth and influence. The way you present and deliver that value determines how it is perceived, how many people it reaches, and ultimately how much impact it generates. Two people can solve the same problem, but the one who packages their solution more effectively will almost always be rewarded more. Packaging turns an idea into an experience and transforms raw usefulness into something people recognize, trust, and are willing to invest in.

Why Packaging Matters

Value on its own is invisible until it is communicated. A brilliant product, service, or insight cannot create results if no one understands why it matters. Packaging bridges that gap. It helps people grasp the transformation you are offering and positions it in a way that connects with their priorities. Without this, even the most valuable solutions risk being overlooked.

Packaging is not about exaggeration or manipulation; it is about clarity and resonance. The goal is to help others see what you have created as the obvious answer to a pressing need. When you package value well, you reduce friction in decision-making. People feel confident engaging with what you offer because they understand it immediately and trust that it will deliver.

Aligning Packaging With Perception

How value is framed affects how it is received. A solution that feels vague or generic rarely inspires commitment, even if it is effective. By contrast, a solution that feels tailored, specific, and outcome-driven creates urgency and desire. This is why presentation — from the words you choose to the format you use — is as important as the underlying content.

Perception is shaped by details: the professionalism of your materials, the clarity of your message, and the emotions your story evokes. High-value packaging signals high-value solutions. It tells people that you respect their time and understand their problem deeply. When done right, packaging is not decoration; it is part of the value itself.

Making Value Tangible

One challenge in offering solutions is that many forms of value are intangible. Peace of mind, confidence, efficiency — these are real benefits, yet they can be hard to quantify. Effective packaging turns intangible outcomes into concrete promises. This could involve illustrating before-and-after scenarios, showing measurable results, or providing testimonials that demonstrate real-world impact.

When people can visualize the change your solution creates, they are more willing to commit. Tangibility reduces uncertainty and shifts focus from cost to return. Instead of questioning whether they should invest, they begin imagining how their life or business will look after they do.

Choosing the Right Format

Different problems require different formats to deliver solutions effectively. A high-touch service may be ideal for complex, personalized challenges, while a digital product can serve thousands at once. Workshops, memberships, consulting, books, and online courses each package value differently, with varying levels of scalability and intimacy. The best choice depends on your goals, the nature of the problem, and how your audience prefers to engage.

The critical factor is alignment. The format should match both the depth of transformation you are offering and the expectations of those you aim to help. Misalignment — such as offering a one-size-fits-all program for a deeply personal issue — can dilute perceived value and limit results.

Refining how you present value involves simplifying without diluting impact. Complex explanations often confuse rather than convince. The clearer the promise, the easier it is for someone to decide. Clarity does not mean removing depth; it means communicating benefits in a way that makes immediate sense. This is why strong packaging often leads with outcomes rather than features. People want to know what life will look like after using your solution, not just what it contains.

A crucial element of effective packaging is trust. Even the best offer will be questioned if people are unsure about credibility. Building trust requires transparency, consistency, and proof. Testimonials, case studies, and demonstrations all help illustrate that your solution delivers what it claims.

At the same time, honesty about limitations creates respect. Overpromising may lead to short-term interest, but it damages long-term relationships and reputation.

Experience is another layer of packaging that significantly impacts perception. How people feel during every interaction — from first contact to follow-up — becomes part of the value. A seamless, thoughtful experience communicates care and professionalism. This can be as simple as clear instructions, responsive communication, or thoughtful design that reduces friction. When people feel understood and supported, they perceive higher value and are more likely to commit fully to what you offer.

Differentiation is essential in crowded markets. Many solutions compete for attention, but few stand out. To differentiate, focus on what makes your approach uniquely suited to solve the problem. This might be a method you developed, a perspective shaped by your experience, or a combination of skills others do not have. Differentiation is not about being louder; it is about being unmistakably aligned with the need you address in a way no one else replicates.

Positioning also plays a significant role in perceived value. The same solution can be seen as premium or disposable depending on how it is framed. Price is part of this perception, but so are context and presentation. A clear narrative about why your solution matters, who it is for, and what it delivers elevates it beyond a commodity. When people understand the story behind your work, they connect emotionally and see greater meaning in what they are investing in.

Sustainability must be considered as well. Packaging that promises transformation must deliver consistently over time. If the delivery of value cannot scale or maintain quality as demand grows, trust erodes. This is why building systems to support delivery is as important as creating the solution itself. Thoughtful packaging considers the long-term experience, ensuring people receive not only what they expect but also ongoing benefits that reinforce loyalty.

Ultimately, packaging value for maximum impact is about alignment — between the problem you solve, the audience you serve, and the way you present your solution. When this alignment is achieved, value becomes visible, compelling, and scalable. People recognize not only what you offer but why it matters, and that clarity transforms both your ability to help others and your capacity to build lasting wealth from the impact you create.

Part III. Escaping the 9–5 Trap and Building Wealth

Breaking free from the traditional 9–5 grind is not just about quitting a job; it is about creating a life where your income and freedom are no longer dictated by someone else's schedule. For many, the idea of escaping this cycle feels impossible. The security of a steady paycheck is comforting, but that comfort often comes at the cost of growth, autonomy, and the ability to build real wealth. This section is designed to help you navigate that shift — moving from dependence on fixed wages to designing systems and strategies that generate income on your terms.

The 9–5 structure was built for predictability, not abundance. It rewards reliability, not necessarily impact. You trade time for money, and no matter how hard you work, your earnings are capped by the position you hold. This model can cover expenses, but it rarely creates the leverage required for financial freedom. Understanding this limitation is the first step toward building something better. It is not about rejecting employment entirely — for many, a job can fund the transition — but about refusing to let it define your ceiling.

Escaping this trap begins with mindset but does not end there. A new perspective must be paired with practical action: learning how to identify opportunities that create disproportionate value, how to turn skills into assets, and how to structure income in ways that continue to grow even when you are not working. These strategies demand patience and discipline but reward you with a level of control and scalability that traditional employment cannot offer.

This part of the book will guide you through that process. You will see how to reframe your skills and experiences into assets that others find valuable, how to navigate the transition from employee to builder, and how to create streams of income that scale without sacrificing quality of life. By the end, you will understand not just how to earn more, but how to design a financial foundation that frees you from trading hours for dollars — a foundation built to last and to grow.

Chapter 5: Breaking the 9–5 Trap

The Hidden Cost of Employment

Employment is often presented as the safest and most responsible path. From a young age, most people are told to get a stable job, climb the ladder, and save steadily for retirement. On the surface, this seems logical: predictable income, benefits, and a clear structure for growth. Yet beneath this apparent security lies a cost that few acknowledge. It is not only financial but also psychological and opportunity-based — a cost that quietly compounds over years and can keep even ambitious individuals stuck in mediocrity.

The Illusion of Stability

A steady paycheck creates the perception of safety. You know exactly what is coming in each month, and you plan your life around that certainty. But this stability is fragile. The moment the company restructures, automates, or shifts priorities, your income can vanish overnight. Unlike owning assets or building scalable systems, employment ties your livelihood to decisions you do not control. In exchange for predictability today, you forfeit flexibility tomorrow.

This trade-off is rarely questioned because the risks of employment are subtle. Layoffs make headlines, but the quieter risks — stagnant wages, capped earning potential, and missed opportunities for growth — are less visible. Over decades, these hidden risks can have a greater impact than any single job loss.

Trading Time Instead of Building Assets

Perhaps the greatest cost of employment is that it locks you into trading time for money. Every dollar earned requires a direct exchange of your hours and energy. When you stop working, the income stops. This linear relationship between effort and reward makes it nearly impossible to create exponential growth. While investments and ownership can compound, hourly work cannot.

This model also places a ceiling on your potential. Even high-paying roles have limits because they are tied to job titles, salary bands, and industry norms. No matter how skilled you are, your compensation is determined more by the structure of the company than by the full value you create. As long as you operate within this system, you remain constrained by its rules.

The Hidden Expenses of Employment

Employment also carries costs that are rarely factored into the paycheck. Commuting, professional wardrobes, and unpaid overtime all eat into earnings. The mental drain of rigid schedules and limited autonomy can lead to stress-related expenses, from health issues to burnout recovery. Even benefits like retirement plans or health insurance, while valuable, are often used to justify lower salaries compared to what you might earn independently.

Opportunity cost is perhaps the most significant hidden expense. Every hour spent working for someone else is an hour not invested in building something of your own. The energy devoted to maintaining your role — meetings, performance reviews, office politics — could instead fuel assets that generate income long after the initial work is done. Over years, this lost compounding potential represents a massive unseen cost.

Over time, the compounding effect of these hidden costs becomes more apparent. Years spent prioritizing job security over personal growth often result in skills that plateau and opportunities that narrow. The longer you remain in a role designed around stability rather than scale, the harder it becomes to imagine alternatives. This is why many people feel trapped in positions they no longer enjoy but fear leaving — the structure that once felt safe begins to feel like a cage.

Another overlooked cost is the psychological conditioning that employment fosters. Most companies are designed to extract maximum value from employees while giving just enough compensation to retain them. Performance metrics and promotions create the illusion of advancement, yet the underlying exchange remains the same: time for money. Even when salaries increase, lifestyle inflation often keeps pace, leaving individuals no closer to financial freedom despite working harder and earning more.

The opportunity cost intensifies when considering what could be built outside of the 9–5 structure. Skills developed on the job are often transferable to independent ventures, yet they remain underutilized because all available energy is consumed by the demands of employment. Side projects, investments, or businesses that could compound over years are postponed indefinitely. The window to experiment narrows, and by the time many realize it, their most flexible and creative years have passed.

There is also the cost of dependence. When your only source of income is a single employer, you place your financial stability entirely in their hands. Economic downturns, corporate restructures, or changes in leadership can alter your future without warning. True security does not come from depending on one paycheck; it comes from diversifying income streams and building systems that continue working regardless of external shifts.

Recognizing these costs does not mean rejecting employment entirely. For many, a job provides essential experience and resources needed to transition into greater independence. The key is to use employment strategically rather than passively. Instead of viewing it as the destination, treat it as a launchpad — a way to acquire skills, fund investments, and build the foundation for something that eventually frees you from the limitations of trading time for money.

This requires a shift in how you evaluate your career. Instead of asking only whether a role pays well, consider what it positions you to build over the long term. Does it allow you to develop expertise others will pay for directly? Does it give you insight into markets where you could later create value? Does it provide the stability needed to invest in assets that generate income outside your paycheck? When you frame employment as part of a bigger plan rather than the entire plan, you begin to reclaim control over your financial trajectory.

Escaping the hidden costs of employment is not about recklessly abandoning a steady job but about gradually reducing dependence on it. By building parallel streams of income, developing assets, and reframing skills for broader use, you create leverage that employment alone cannot provide. Over time, this leverage allows you to step out of the 9–5 trap on your own terms — not because you have to, but because you have built something better.

Building Side Income Ecosystems

Creating a single stream of side income can ease financial stress. Building an ecosystem of income streams, however, changes your entire financial trajectory. An ecosystem is not just multiple random hustles; it is a connected network of skills, assets, and opportunities that support and amplify one another. When designed strategically, each part strengthens the whole, creating resilience and compounding growth over time.

Why Ecosystems Outperform Isolated Hustles

Many people start with a side hustle to earn extra cash — freelancing, selling online, driving for rideshare companies. These efforts can help in the short term but often remain linear. When you stop working, the income stops. Ecosystems are different because they focus on interconnected assets that continue to provide value even when you are not actively trading time. Each piece feeds another, turning temporary projects into sustainable wealth-building frameworks.

An ecosystem approach also reduces risk. Relying on one income stream, even a side business, makes you vulnerable to market changes or personal limitations. A diversified but connected network cushions you against disruptions. If one stream slows, others can carry the weight, keeping you stable while you adjust.

Identifying Core Skills as the Foundation

Every ecosystem begins with a core skill or interest. This is the anchor that informs which income streams make sense and how they can connect. Someone skilled in design might start freelancing, later create digital templates, and eventually launch courses teaching others. A person experienced in fitness might begin coaching clients, create content online, and develop a subscription program. Each step builds on the last rather than starting from scratch.

This approach not only saves energy but also positions you as an authority in a specific space. When your projects share a common theme, your reputation compounds. Clients or audiences from one stream naturally flow into others, creating synergy that scattered efforts cannot replicate.

Balancing Active and Passive Elements

Ecosystems thrive on a balance between active and passive income. Active streams — freelancing, consulting, direct services — generate cash flow quickly and fund the development of more passive assets. Passive elements — investments, digital products, automated businesses — take longer to build but continue earning long after the initial work is done. Combining both ensures you meet short-term needs while building long-term security. The key is progression. Begin with what can generate immediate income, but from the start, design with the goal of eventual leverage. Ask how each project can evolve into something less dependent on constant effort. This mindset prevents burnout and keeps growth sustainable.

The Compounding Effect of Integration

The strength of an ecosystem is in its integration. A single audience can support multiple offers, a single skill can create several products, and a single asset can open doors to new opportunities. Integration allows you to multiply returns without multiplying workload. Instead of managing separate ventures, you create a self-reinforcing system where success in one area boosts success in others.

Designing a side income ecosystem begins with mapping connections rather than stacking unrelated ventures. Start by looking at the skills you already have and the problems you are equipped to solve. From there, identify extensions that naturally flow from each income stream. A freelance writer might create a blog, then repurpose articles into e-books, and later develop a course on writing strategies. Each new stream grows from the previous one, reusing existing assets and audiences rather than building from zero every time.

Testing each layer of the ecosystem before scaling prevents wasted effort. Small experiments — a pilot offer, a minimal viable product, a short consultation series — allow you to gauge interest and refine your approach without overcommitting. Early validation ensures that your ecosystem grows in response to real demand rather than assumptions. This approach is slower at the start but prevents burnout and avoids building structures that collapse under their own complexity.

Scalability should guide every decision. Ask how a stream can evolve to serve more people without proportionally increasing your workload. Can a one-on-one service transition into a group format or an automated program? Can content created once be repurposed across multiple platforms? Can customer relationships lead to referrals or recurring revenue rather than one-time transactions? By consistently seeking ways to expand impact without expanding effort, you set the stage for compounding growth.

Diversification within the ecosystem also strengthens resilience. While the streams should share a common foundation, each should address a slightly different need or audience segment. This way, a market shift in one area does not destabilize the entire system. For example, a fitness coach with in-person training, digital programs, and branded merchandise can pivot focus depending on trends or disruptions, maintaining stability through flexibility. The mindset behind building an ecosystem is as important as the tactics. It requires patience to focus on gradual layering rather than chasing quick wins. It also requires discipline to stay aligned with your core skill or theme, avoiding distractions that dilute focus. Many people sabotage potential ecosystems by scattering energy into unrelated ventures, leaving each underdeveloped. True leverage comes from depth, not breadth — creating multiple income streams that work together rather than competing for your attention.

Sustainability is the final measure of a successful ecosystem. Each stream should not only generate revenue but also fit into the life you are designing. If an income source creates constant stress or pulls you away from what matters, it undermines the freedom you are working toward. Building systems, delegating tasks, and automating wherever possible protect your energy and ensure the ecosystem enhances your life rather than consuming it.

Over time, these interconnected streams form a structure that is both adaptable and scalable. One stream funds another, one audience feeds another, and the skills you refine in one area strengthen your ability to create value elsewhere. This is the quiet advantage of ecosystems: while others chase one-off wins, you are constructing a foundation that compounds with every step forward. It is this foundation that allows you to transition away from dependence on a single paycheck and into a model of wealth-building that grows stronger the longer it runs.

Designing the Transition Plan

Escaping the 9–5 trap and moving into independent wealth creation is not something that happens overnight. It requires a deliberate and well-structured transition plan. Without one, the shift can feel overwhelming or risky, often leading people to either stay stuck in employment or leap too soon without a safety net. A carefully designed plan allows you to manage risk, build momentum, and create confidence in every step you take toward financial independence.

Establishing a Clear Destination

A transition plan starts by defining what freedom means to you. Financial independence looks different for everyone. For some, it might mean replacing a salary with entrepreneurial income; for others, it might mean having multiple side income streams that together cover living expenses. Clarity on your goal shapes every decision that follows — how much income you need, how long the transition should take, and what skills or assets you must develop along the way.

Begin by calculating your baseline. Know exactly how much money you need to cover essentials, how much you want to invest in future growth, and what level of lifestyle you are aiming for. This number becomes the benchmark for your transition strategy. Without it, you risk either leaving too soon and facing financial stress or waiting far longer than necessary.

Building the Financial Buffer

A core element of any transition is creating a financial cushion. This buffer provides psychological safety and practical flexibility. It allows you to take calculated risks without the constant pressure of immediate income replacement. While the exact size depends on your personal risk tolerance and responsibilities, a common target is saving several months of essential expenses before reducing or leaving traditional employment.

The buffer is not only about covering costs; it is about creating breathing room to experiment. Building side income takes time, and early stages often involve testing offers, refining systems, and facing setbacks. A reserve ensures you can navigate this phase without panic-driven decisions that compromise your long-term vision.

Leveraging Employment Strategically

Employment can serve as an asset during your transition rather than an obstacle. The goal is to use your current role to fund and accelerate your shift instead of viewing it as wasted time. This means approaching work with intentionality — maximizing income where possible, learning skills that will translate into your next phase, and using predictable hours to structure consistent progress on side ventures outside of work.

Rather than quitting abruptly, many find it more effective to scale back gradually. This might involve reducing hours, shifting to freelance work, or negotiating flexible arrangements as side income grows. A phased exit reduces pressure and helps ensure the new income streams are sustainable before you rely on them fully.

Milestones are essential for managing a smooth transition. Without them, it is easy to either rush forward too quickly or linger in preparation for years. Each milestone represents a measurable step, such as achieving a specific savings target, securing a certain level of side income, or completing a skill-building phase. These benchmarks provide clarity and allow you to evaluate whether you are ready for the next stage rather than relying on vague feelings of readiness.

Breaking the process into stages also creates motivation. Reaching each milestone builds confidence and reinforces that progress is being made, even if the final goal still feels distant. This psychological boost is crucial during the middle stages, when initial excitement begins to fade and challenges start to surface.

Focus is another critical element. A transition can easily become overwhelming if you attempt too many changes at once — building side income, reducing expenses, learning new skills, and planning the exit simultaneously. Prioritizing one major objective at a time keeps energy directed where it will create the greatest leverage. Often, this means first stabilizing personal finances, then establishing one strong income stream, and only later diversifying into additional ventures.

Energy management is as important as financial planning. Many people underestimate the physical and mental toll of balancing a job with building something on the side. Burnout can derail even the best-designed strategy. Creating realistic schedules, setting boundaries around rest, and using structured planning tools helps maintain momentum without sacrificing health or relationships. This transition is a marathon, not a sprint, and pacing yourself increases the likelihood of sustained success.

Systemizing tasks wherever possible reduces decision fatigue and accelerates growth. Simple frameworks, like weekly reviews of progress and automated financial tracking, prevent chaos from creeping in as responsibilities multiply. The more you can create repeatable processes for marketing, content creation, or client management, the less energy you spend reinventing the wheel. Systems are what turn scattered side projects into cohesive businesses capable of scaling beyond your personal capacity.

As you near the final stages of transition, the focus shifts from preparation to execution. This is when you test whether your side income can consistently cover essential expenses and whether your systems are strong enough to handle growth without constant oversight. If gaps remain, address them while still employed rather than after leaving. The goal is to step away from the paycheck with stability, not desperation.

The final decision to leave traditional employment should feel less like a leap and more like a natural progression. By the time you reach this point, your savings, income streams, and systems should provide enough security that the move feels inevitable rather than risky. This confidence comes not from luck but from careful planning and repeated validation at every stage of the journey.

A well-designed transition plan is not only about replacing income; it is about reshaping identity. As you move from employee to independent creator of wealth, you will adopt new habits, responsibilities, and perspectives. The process itself becomes transformative, preparing you not just to escape the 9–5, but to thrive in the freedom and opportunities that follow.

Chapter 6: The Hidden Codes of the Wealthy

How the Elite See Money Differently

The wealthiest individuals operate under a fundamentally different framework when it comes to money. While most people think in terms of earning and spending, the elite view money as a tool for leverage, influence, and long-term positioning. Their decisions are rarely reactive. Instead, they are guided by principles that allow them to turn opportunities into systems, and systems into enduring wealth. Understanding this mindset shift is essential if you want to step beyond conventional financial thinking and start building on the same principles.

Money as Energy, Not Just Currency

For the average person, money is seen purely as a medium of exchange — something earned from work and spent on needs or desires. The elite view it as energy that can be directed to multiply itself. They do not ask, "What can I buy?" but "Where can this flow to create the most return?" This shift leads to decisions that prioritize investment over consumption and growth over immediate gratification.

This is why the wealthy often appear less concerned with the cost of things in the short term. Their focus is on the potential of every dollar to generate more dollars. A hundred dollars spent on entertainment is gone forever; a hundred dollars placed in the right investment can create streams of income that continue long after the initial outlay.

The Power of Asymmetric Returns

One of the most striking differences in perspective is how the elite approach risk. Most people avoid risk entirely, equating safety with keeping money untouched. The wealthy look for asymmetric opportunities — situations where the potential upside far outweighs the downside. This does not mean reckless bets; it means carefully analyzing scenarios where limited risk can lead to exponential reward.

This principle explains why elite investors often allocate resources to startups, real estate, or new technologies. While many of these ventures fail, a single success can cover losses and create massive growth. They understand that wealth is built not by avoiding all risk but by structuring it intelligently.

Playing the Long Game

The average financial mindset is focused on short-term cycles — paychecks, monthly bills, annual raises. The elite think in decades. They design strategies that may take years to bear fruit but create lasting impact when they do. This is why they prioritize assets over income. Assets, whether businesses, intellectual property, or investments, continue to produce value over time, often compounding quietly in the background.

This long view also affects how they handle setbacks. Where most people panic at losses, the elite treat them as part of the process. They understand that temporary downturns often precede breakthroughs and that patience is as valuable as strategy. This resilience is rooted in confidence that systems, not single events, determine outcomes over the long haul.

Controlling the Game, Not Just Playing It

Another defining trait is the focus on control. Most people participate in markets passively — they invest in funds, work for companies, or follow trends created by others. The elite aim to control the levers of value creation. They build businesses rather than simply work for them, create products rather than only consume them, and influence markets rather than merely react to them.

Control does not always mean ownership of everything. It often means having influence at critical points — owning the platform, the distribution channel, or the intellectual property that others rely on. This positioning allows them to set terms rather than accept them, which over time compounds their advantage.

A defining feature of elite thinking is their focus on liquidity and optionality. Liquidity refers to having access to resources that can be deployed quickly when opportunities arise. While many people tie up all their funds in fixed expenses or illiquid assets, the wealthy deliberately maintain cash reserves or easily accessible capital. This flexibility allows them to move fast when an undervalued investment or unique deal appears, positioning themselves ahead of those who need time to reorganize their finances.

Optionality complements liquidity by preserving the ability to choose. Rather than locking themselves into rigid paths, the elite create structures that allow for pivoting. This could mean keeping investments diversified, maintaining multiple income streams, or designing businesses that can adapt to shifts in the market. Optionality ensures that when circumstances change — and they always do — they are not trapped by a single plan but can redirect their energy toward the best available path.

Daily decisions reflect this broader philosophy. Where most people evaluate purchases based on cost alone, the wealthy consider opportunity cost. They ask whether a purchase will generate returns, improve their capabilities, or enhance their network. Even leisure spending is often intentional, serving as an avenue for building relationships or gaining insights that later pay dividends. This is not to say they never indulge, but even indulgence is balanced with a long-term view of how each choice fits into their larger strategy.

Another distinction is their approach to income itself. Instead of relying solely on active work, the elite prioritize building systems that generate income independent of their direct effort. They view money earned passively — through investments, royalties, or automated businesses — as the ultimate measure of freedom. This shift from labor to leverage is what allows them to scale wealth without sacrificing quality of life. They invest early in creating assets that continue to produce long after the initial work is complete.

Networking also plays a significant role in their financial perspective. The elite understand that relationships often unlock opportunities faster than pure capital. They intentionally cultivate connections with people who operate at high levels of influence or insight. These relationships are not purely transactional; they are built on shared value, trust, and mutual benefit. Over time, such networks create access to deals, partnerships, and knowledge that remain out of reach for those who operate in isolation.

Perhaps most importantly, the wealthy view money as a tool for freedom rather than as an end goal. Accumulating wealth for its own sake holds little appeal; the true objective is the autonomy it provides. Freedom to choose where to live, how to work, and what to focus on becomes the ultimate measure of success. This orientation prevents them from chasing trends blindly and instead anchors decisions in personal priorities and values.

Adopting this mindset does not require vast sums of capital. It begins with rethinking how you measure value, how you view risk, and how you position yourself to act when opportunities arise. By shifting focus from short-term security to long-term control, you begin to play the same game the elite have mastered — one where wealth is not just earned, but engineered for lasting impact and freedom.

Networks and Social Capital

Wealth is rarely built in isolation. Behind every significant success story is a network of relationships that provided insight, opportunity, or direct collaboration. Money and skills matter, but access to the right people often multiplies their impact. This is the essence of social capital — the value that comes from trust, reputation, and the connections you cultivate over time.

The Invisible Currency of Relationships

Social capital functions like an invisible currency. It cannot be measured on a balance sheet, yet it influences financial outcomes as strongly as any investment. The wealthiest individuals understand that who you know often determines what you can access: unique opportunities, better terms on deals, introductions to influential decision-makers, and faster solutions to problems that would take others years to solve.

Unlike financial capital, social capital grows through mutual benefit rather than direct transactions. It is earned by consistently adding value to others, building trust, and maintaining authenticity. This makes it accessible to anyone willing to approach networking with intention rather than superficiality.

Moving Beyond Traditional Networking

Many people associate networking with forced conversations and handing out business cards at events. This view misses the deeper purpose of building relationships. True networks are not about collecting contacts but creating connections rooted in shared goals or values. The goal is not immediate gain but long-term reciprocity — helping others in ways that naturally lead to opportunities flowing back over time.

This shift from transactional to relational thinking transforms how you approach people. Instead of asking, "What can I get from this person?" the better question is, "How can I create value for them?" Over time, this approach leads to genuine trust, which is the foundation of meaningful social capital.

The Compounding Effect of Social Capital

Social capital compounds much like financial investments. A single introduction can lead to a chain of opportunities: a new client, a strategic partner, an investor, or a mentor who accelerates your growth. Each connection you nurture strengthens your reputation and expands your reach, often opening doors you never knew existed.

This compounding is why small, consistent efforts in relationship-building can outperform aggressive short-term networking. Checking in with contacts, offering insights, and connecting people with each other builds goodwill that grows quietly in the background until a pivotal moment arises.

The Role of Reputation

Reputation is the backbone of social capital. It determines how people talk about you when you are not in the room and whether they are willing to stake their credibility on recommending you. A strong reputation is built on reliability, expertise, and integrity. Even one breach of trust can damage years of relationship-building, so protecting your reputation is as important as growing your network.

Reputation also shapes the type of opportunities you attract. High-quality relationships tend to cluster; once you are seen as trustworthy and capable within one circle, referrals naturally flow from that credibility into others.

Expanding social capital begins with intentionality rather than volume. A small circle of high-quality relationships is far more powerful than hundreds of shallow connections. Identifying the circles you want to grow into — industries, communities, or interest groups aligned with your goals — allows you to focus energy where it creates meaningful outcomes. This does not mean seeking only people who can benefit you directly, but rather surrounding yourself with those who share ambition, integrity, and a willingness to collaborate.

Creating value for others is the fastest way to strengthen connections. Offering insights, sharing resources, or making introductions without expectation builds goodwill and positions you as someone worth knowing. Over time, people begin to associate your name with solutions rather than requests, which naturally leads them to include you in opportunities. This principle works whether you are networking with peers, mentors, or potential partners: generosity, when genuine, creates reciprocity.

Depth matters as much as breadth. It is easy to collect names, but influence grows through trust built over repeated interactions. Investing time in understanding others' goals and challenges creates stronger bonds than simply appearing at events. A single meaningful conversation can be more valuable than dozens of casual exchanges. This is why following up, staying in touch, and checking in without an agenda are critical. Relationships that endure are nurtured, not rushed.

Positioning yourself in the right environments accelerates this process. Communities that align with your vision — masterminds, professional groups, volunteer initiatives — naturally attract individuals who think beyond conventional limits. Proximity to such people shifts your perspective and raises your standards, often challenging you to grow faster than you would alone. The conversations you have in these spaces spark insights and opportunities that cannot be found in isolation.

Maintaining integrity is essential for sustaining social capital. Overpromising, failing to deliver, or approaching relationships with hidden agendas erodes trust quickly. In contrast, consistently showing up, honoring commitments, and being transparent about intentions builds a reputation that precedes you. This reputation becomes a silent advocate, opening doors even when you are not present to knock.

As your network expands, leverage it thoughtfully. Introductions should be mutually beneficial, not forced. Recommendations should protect both your credibility and that of the people you connect. Thoughtful curation of relationships ensures that the value you create strengthens everyone involved rather than diluting trust.

Over time, a well-cultivated network evolves into an ecosystem. Ideas, resources, and opportunities flow naturally between members, creating collective momentum greater than any individual effort. This ecosystem not only supports personal success but also enables you to create impact on a larger scale — mentoring others, building collaborations, and shaping the very environments you once sought to enter.

Social capital grows quietly yet exponentially. Each authentic connection you form today lays the groundwork for opportunities you cannot yet predict. By approaching relationships with long-term vision, generosity, and integrity, you transform networking from a task into an enduring asset —

one that compounds in value just as powerfully as financial capital, fueling both your personal growth and the wealth you aim to create.

The Law of Asymmetric Bets

Building wealth rarely happens through incremental gains alone. The most significant leaps occur when you place yourself in situations where the potential upside is disproportionately larger than the potential downside. This principle, known as the law of asymmetric bets, is a core strategy used by many of the world's wealthiest individuals and investors. It allows them to capitalize on opportunities without exposing themselves to catastrophic loss, transforming calculated risks into engines of exponential growth.

Understanding Asymmetry

An asymmetric bet is any decision where the reward far exceeds the risk. Most people unconsciously make symmetric bets, where the potential loss equals or outweighs the potential gain. For example, working overtime for slightly higher pay is a symmetric bet — more effort yields slightly more income, but the cost to time and energy is significant. In contrast, investing in a skill that permanently increases your earning potential, or in a project that could return multiples of your initial input, is asymmetric.

This principle reframes how you evaluate opportunities. Instead of asking, "What can I gain?" you ask, "What is the worst that can happen, and can I handle it?" If the worst outcome is manageable and the best outcome is transformative, the decision often becomes clear.

Why Most People Miss These Opportunities

Asymmetric bets are widely misunderstood because they often appear unconventional or uncertain. They rarely come labeled as "safe" or "guaranteed," which makes them uncomfortable for those conditioned to avoid risk. Traditional financial advice often encourages minimizing losses at all costs, focusing on steady returns rather than outsized gains. While this approach protects against downside, it also prevents exposure to the kind of opportunities that can accelerate wealth creation.

Fear of failure plays a significant role in this hesitation. Many people overestimate the cost of failure and underestimate their ability to recover. This mindset leads to missed chances — passing on a small investment in a promising venture, declining to learn a new skill, or hesitating to launch a side project that could change their financial trajectory.

The Mathematics of Asymmetry

To illustrate, consider a scenario where you risk $100 with the potential to earn $1,000. Even if you succeed only once out of ten attempts, you break even. Anything beyond that is profit. This is the power of asymmetric thinking: the downside is limited, but the upside is exponential. The wealthy understand that they do not need every bet to succeed. They only need a few big wins to compensate for the small losses along the way.

This is why venture capitalists, for example, invest in multiple startups knowing most will fail. A single breakout success can return the entire fund and more. While the average person might see failure in the majority of those investments, the investor sees success in the overall portfolio's asymmetric potential.

Recognizing Asymmetric Bets in Daily Life

Asymmetry is not limited to high finance. It shows up in everyday decisions. Learning a skill like public speaking, negotiating, or digital marketing requires modest time and effort compared to the lifelong benefits it provides. Starting a low-cost online business, experimenting with content creation, or investing in an undervalued market during a downturn are all examples of asymmetric bets when approached strategically.

Identifying asymmetric opportunities begins with sharpening your perception of value. Most people evaluate options based only on cost or immediate payoff, overlooking factors like scalability, compounding benefits, and secondary advantages. The key is to look beyond surface metrics and ask what the upside could become over time. A modest investment in a skill might not seem life-changing today, but if it permanently increases your earning power, the return is far greater than its initial cost suggests.

Clarity comes from assessing the worst-case scenario first. If you can tolerate the downside, you free yourself to focus on the upside without paralyzing fear. This mental framework helps you pursue bold opportunities without reckless exposure. For example, starting a side project that costs little more than your time is low-risk but carries the potential to grow into a significant income stream. By repeatedly taking these calculated swings, you stack the odds of a breakthrough in your favor.

Managing emotions is crucial, as asymmetric bets often involve uncertainty and delayed gratification. There will be moments where progress feels invisible or where small failures test your resolve. Understanding that losses are part of the process reframes them as tuition for future wins rather than signs of defeat. The elite are not immune to setbacks; they simply expect them and structure their approach so that one win pays for many losses.

Positioning is another factor that determines whether an opportunity can truly be asymmetric. Being early in a trend, acquiring knowledge others overlook, or building relationships in underexplored markets can create outsized advantages. The same bet placed at the wrong time or without the right preparation may lose its edge. This is why continuous learning and staying attuned to shifts in technology, culture, and economics are essential. Those who anticipate change rather than react to it consistently find opportunities others miss.

Structuring bets for asymmetry involves spreading them across multiple avenues rather than placing everything on one outcome. This portfolio mindset allows small failures without derailing your overall trajectory. Each attempt provides feedback, skill development, and connections that improve future decisions. Over time, the cumulative effect of many small bets compounds into major breakthroughs.

The law of asymmetric bets is not about constant gambling; it is about selective boldness. You are deliberately seeking situations where the payoff transforms your life without requiring life-threatening risk. This principle applies whether you are investing, launching a business, or pivoting your career. Each decision is guided by the same question: does the potential reward justify the minimal cost of entry?

Mastering this way of thinking gradually shifts how you see every choice. You stop chasing incremental gains and begin building leverage. You no longer fear calculated risks, because you understand that wealth is rarely created through perfect certainty but through a series of imperfect yet intelligent decisions. Over time, these decisions reshape not just your finances but your identity, positioning you as someone capable of spotting and seizing opportunities that others never recognize.

Part IV. Integrating the Hidden Codes

By this point, you have explored the mindset shifts, strategies, and frameworks that separate ordinary financial thinking from the patterns used by those who quietly build extraordinary wealth. You have seen how value creation matters more than time, how networks amplify opportunity, and how asymmetric bets accelerate growth. These are not isolated tactics. They are interconnected codes — pieces of a system that, when combined, create an entirely new approach to wealth and freedom.

Integration is where transformation begins. Knowledge alone changes little. Many people read about financial strategies but remain stuck because they fail to connect concepts into a cohesive whole. They treat ideas as separate experiments rather than parts of a unified plan. This final part is designed to bridge that gap. It will show you how to layer everything you have learned into daily habits, long-term decisions, and a personal philosophy that endures.

The process of integration requires alignment between thought, action, and identity. It is no longer enough to know the principles intellectually; they must become the lens through which you evaluate every opportunity and challenge. This means reshaping not just what you do with money but how you see yourself in relation to it. Moving from consumer to creator. From participant to architect. From reactive to intentional.

Integration is also about sustainability. Wealth built on scattered effort or constant hustle rarely lasts. The systems you create must support growth without burning you out or compromising what matters most. When the hidden codes are fully integrated, they stop feeling like strategies you have to force. They become instinctive — guiding your choices quietly in the background and freeing your energy for higher-level pursuits.

This part will help you solidify that shift. It will focus on connecting the principles into a cohesive operating system, building structures that reinforce themselves, and preparing you to adapt as circumstances evolve. The goal is not just to finish this book with inspiration but to leave with a new framework for how you live, earn, and invest — a framework that continues to serve you long after you turn the last page.

Chapter 7: Mastering Cash Flow and Capital

From Paycheck-to-Paycheck to Cash Flow Positive

Living paycheck to paycheck is one of the most common financial traps. Even people who earn well can find themselves caught in it, constantly waiting for the next deposit to cover bills, with little left over to invest or save. This cycle creates chronic stress, limits opportunities, and keeps you reactive instead of proactive. Breaking free from it is not about extreme frugality or luck; it is about re-engineering how money flows through your life so that you always operate from a position of surplus rather than scarcity.

Understanding the Paycheck-to-Paycheck Trap

This cycle persists not simply because of low income, but because expenses expand to match earnings. As people earn more, their lifestyle often scales with it: bigger homes, newer cars, higher subscriptions, and spontaneous spending justified by "I can afford it now." Over time, this expansion leaves little buffer, meaning any unexpected cost — a car repair, medical bill, or even a missed paycheck — triggers panic.

The deeper issue is a lack of intentional structure. Without a system for managing money, most people default to short-term thinking. They focus on covering immediate obligations rather than directing funds toward building cash flow and assets. This reactive mindset feeds the cycle, ensuring each month feels like starting over.

The Shift Toward Cash Flow Positive

Becoming cash flow positive is not just about earning more; it is about creating a consistent gap between what comes in and what goes out, then using that gap to build momentum. This surplus, even if modest at first, becomes the seed for savings, investments, and eventually wealth. The focus shifts from survival to strategy. You stop asking, "Can I afford this?" and begin asking, "How do I make my money work harder for me?"

The first step is clarity. Most people underestimate how much they spend or misjudge where their money actually goes. Tracking expenses for even one month often reveals patterns and leaks that were invisible before. Awareness alone can lead to immediate improvement, as you start questioning purchases that no longer align with your goals.

Controlling Outflow Without Sacrificing Quality of Life

Cutting expenses does not mean living in deprivation. It means aligning spending with priorities and eliminating costs that add little value. Many recurring expenses — unused subscriptions, impulse buys, convenience fees — can be removed without impacting quality of life. Redirecting even a small portion of these funds toward debt repayment or savings creates momentum that compounds over time.

The goal is to create enough breathing room to stop relying on credit cards or payday loans to bridge gaps. This shift immediately reduces financial stress and begins building confidence. As this surplus grows, it can be deployed toward opportunities rather than emergencies, which is the foundation of financial freedom.

Increasing Inflow Strategically

While expense control creates the initial gap, increasing income accelerates the journey. This does not always require changing jobs; it can come from leveraging existing skills in freelance work, pursuing performance-based pay increases, or building side income streams. The critical factor is directing the extra income toward long-term goals rather than allowing lifestyle creep to erase the progress.

Turning a surplus into a structured system ensures progress is not temporary. Many people manage to cut costs or boost income briefly, but without a plan that directs extra cash automatically, habits revert and the cycle repeats. Automating the flow of money is critical. Allocating portions of each paycheck to savings, investments, and essential expenses before discretionary spending removes constant decision fatigue and helps new behaviors stick. What starts as discipline eventually becomes routine, requiring less willpower over time.

A priority for early surplus is building a basic emergency reserve. This cushion transforms financial resilience. Even a few weeks of expenses in cash reduces anxiety and prevents reliance on high-interest debt when surprises arise. Once this reserve is established, momentum builds because you no longer drain energy reacting to crises. You can shift focus toward paying down obligations that weigh on cash flow, such as high-interest credit cards or personal loans, which frees even more income each month. Debt elimination should be approached strategically rather than emotionally. Focusing on the most expensive debt first often yields the fastest financial relief. Each balance cleared not only improves monthly cash flow but also builds psychological momentum. Every win reinforces that forward motion is possible, replacing feelings of helplessness with confidence in your ability to change course.

As cash flow improves, the next step is creating buckets for future goals rather than letting funds sit aimlessly. Dividing surplus between short-term needs, medium-term opportunities, and long-term investments ensures balanced growth. Short-term funds cover near-future expenses or planned purchases, reducing the temptation to use credit. Medium-term funds can seed projects like starting a side business. Long-term funds, directed into investments or retirement accounts, build enduring wealth.

Shifting from a reactive to proactive stance also means rethinking how you view extra income. Windfalls, bonuses, or unexpected gains are often treated as spending opportunities rather than accelerators of financial goals. Redirecting these toward reserves, debt payoff, or investments dramatically shortens the timeline to financial stability. This approach turns what would have been temporary relief into lasting improvement.

The final layer is building mechanisms that prevent slipping back into old patterns. Regular financial reviews, even just monthly, help ensure spending aligns with priorities and that incremental lifestyle upgrades do not quietly erase progress. These check-ins also create space to celebrate milestones — clearing a credit card, saving a first thousand dollars, or achieving the first month where investments outpace expenses. Acknowledging progress reinforces the new identity you are building: someone in control of their money rather than controlled by it.

Reaching cash flow positive is more than a numerical milestone; it is a psychological one. It marks the shift from surviving to planning, from fearing bills to seeking opportunities. Once that shift happens, financial growth accelerates. You have space to think long-term, to invest with patience, and to pursue opportunities that once felt out of reach. This foundation is what every other wealth-building strategy rests on, and once secured, it permanently alters how you navigate the game of money.

The Power of Capital Positioning

Capital is more than money sitting in a bank account. It is potential energy waiting to be directed. The way you position that capital — where you hold it, how you allocate it, and when you deploy it — can dramatically influence both the speed and scale of your financial growth. Many people focus on how much capital they can accumulate, yet overlook how its positioning determines the opportunities they can access and the risks they can withstand.

Why Positioning Matters as Much as Amount

Two people with the same savings can experience radically different outcomes depending on how those funds are structured. One may have cash scattered across checking accounts with no clear plan, while the other keeps a portion liquid for quick moves, a portion in low-risk reserves, and a portion already earning through investments. The difference is not in total dollars but in strategic placement. Well-positioned capital acts as a springboard, ready to seize opportunities others cannot even consider.

Positioning also affects timing. Opportunity often appears briefly and unexpectedly. Undervalued assets, market shifts, or unique deals reward those who can act quickly. If all your resources are tied up in illiquid investments or locked in commitments, you cannot respond in time. Conversely, if everything sits idle, you miss out on growth. Striking the balance between accessibility and productivity is the essence of effective capital positioning.

Layers of Capital

A powerful approach is to think of capital in layers. The first layer is liquidity — cash or equivalents you can access immediately without penalty. This layer is not about earning high returns; it is about flexibility and peace of mind. It covers emergencies and allows decisive action when opportunities arise.

The second layer is stability — funds allocated to low- or moderate-risk vehicles that preserve value and provide predictable returns. This layer ensures you remain grounded even in volatile conditions. It also supports medium-term goals, bridging the gap between immediate security and long-term growth.

The third layer is growth — capital placed in assets with higher potential returns, such as equities, real estate, or business ventures. These carry more risk but also create the possibility for transformative outcomes. Positioning growth capital wisely ensures it does not jeopardize your foundation while still enabling meaningful wealth creation.

Avoiding the Extremes

Many fall into two extremes when handling capital: hoarding cash out of fear or chasing aggressive returns without safeguards. Both approaches create vulnerability. Excessive cash loses value to inflation and misses compounding opportunities. Overexposure to risk can lead to setbacks that take years to recover from. Balanced positioning allows you to maintain stability while still participating in growth.

Capital positioning is not static. As income, goals, and market conditions evolve, so must your allocations. What makes sense early in wealth building — heavy emphasis on liquidity and skill development — shifts over time toward greater investment and legacy building. The ability to adjust without abandoning discipline separates those who plateau from those who continue advancing.

Repositioning capital effectively requires constant awareness of both personal goals and external conditions. Markets shift, industries rise and fall, and personal circumstances evolve. A static plan that worked last year may no longer be optimal today. This is why regular reviews are critical. Evaluating where your funds sit, whether they are underperforming, and whether new opportunities justify reallocation keeps your capital aligned with your priorities rather than drifting with habit.

Signals for redeployment often appear during moments of imbalance. Excess cash accumulating in low-yield accounts might indicate an opportunity to redirect funds toward higher-return assets. Conversely, overexposure to volatile investments during uncertain economic periods might call for shifting some capital back into reserves. The goal is not constant movement but deliberate adjustments that preserve flexibility while keeping growth in motion.

A useful approach is to anchor decisions in ratios rather than fixed amounts. Instead of targeting a specific dollar figure for liquidity, aim for a percentage of total capital based on your stage of life and risk tolerance. As your wealth grows, these percentages can shift — perhaps starting with a heavy focus on liquidity and gradually tilting toward growth as your foundation strengthens. This method ensures your capital structure evolves naturally alongside your capacity to absorb risk.

Positioning also involves anticipating rather than merely reacting. Those who prepare in advance are better equipped to act when opportunities arise. Building reserves before a market downturn, for instance, allows you to buy undervalued assets while others are retreating. Similarly, preparing funds for an upcoming business venture or real estate purchase ensures you can move quickly when the right deal surfaces. Anticipation transforms timing from guesswork into strategy.

Tax efficiency is another dimension often overlooked in capital positioning. Where you hold money — in taxable accounts, retirement accounts, or vehicles with specific advantages — can significantly influence long-term growth. Optimizing placement can free up additional resources without requiring more income, simply by reducing unnecessary drag on returns. While this requires research or professional guidance, the payoff is substantial over decades.

Psychological factors matter as much as strategy. Poor positioning often stems from fear or impatience rather than lack of knowledge. Holding too much cash because of anxiety about markets, or chasing high-risk opportunities out of frustration with slow progress, both reflect emotional decisions. Creating a structured plan with clear roles for each layer of capital helps remove emotion from the process. You know why each dollar is where it is and what purpose it serves.

Ultimately, capital positioning is about readiness. It places you in a posture of strength, able to weather setbacks without panic and seize opportunities without hesitation. When your money is structured intentionally, you stop feeling reactive and start operating as a strategist. This shift transforms wealth-building from a series of isolated decisions into a cohesive, ongoing process. Over time, that structure compounds, allowing you to grow faster, recover quicker, and navigate uncertainty with the confidence of someone who is always prepared for what comes next.

Stacking and Redeploying Profits

Generating profit is only the first milestone in building lasting wealth. What you do with those profits determines whether they evaporate in consumption or compound into greater opportunities. The practice of stacking and redeploying profits is what transforms occasional wins into consistent growth. Instead of treating profit as an endpoint, you turn it into raw material for the next stage of advancement, creating a cycle where each success funds the next.

Why Stacking Profits Matters

Most people treat extra income as disposable. A bonus at work, a profitable side hustle, or a successful investment often leads to immediate lifestyle upgrades. This tendency, known as lifestyle creep, keeps individuals stuck in the same financial position regardless of their earnings. Stacking profits breaks this cycle by intentionally reserving gains rather than absorbing them into expenses. It is a mindset shift from "I earned it, I can spend it" to "I earned it, now how do I multiply it?"

Stacking profits creates optionality. By accumulating resources, you gain the ability to act when high-quality opportunities arise. Without this reserve, even the best chances for growth slip by because you are unprepared to move. Over time, stacked profits become a form of leverage, allowing you to invest at a higher level and with greater confidence.

The Discipline of Separation

Effective stacking begins with separating profits from regular income and expenses. When gains remain in the same pool as daily finances, they are easily consumed without intention. Creating distinct accounts or allocations for profit ensures clarity and prevents impulsive decisions. This separation signals to yourself that these funds are for building, not spending.

Discipline is key during this phase. The temptation to reward yourself after a win is natural, but overindulgence undermines momentum. This does not mean eliminating enjoyment entirely; rather, it means adopting a ratio where most gains are reinvested while a smaller portion can be set aside for personal reward. This balance sustains motivation without derailing long-term goals.

Timing the Redeployment

Redeploying profits requires patience and strategic timing. Not every surplus should be immediately reinvested; holding until the right opportunity emerges can yield far greater returns. This approach mirrors how skilled investors wait for favorable market conditions rather than forcing action out of restlessness. Having stacked reserves allows you to be selective rather than desperate.

Redeployment also benefits from diversification. Instead of reinvesting all profits into the same vehicle, consider spreading them across complementary opportunities — building multiple layers of growth that support each other. For example, profits from a freelance business might first cover tools that improve efficiency, then flow into investments that generate passive income. Each move builds upon the last, gradually creating a network of assets rather than a single point of failure.

Stacking becomes most powerful when paired with intentional feedback loops. Each reinvestment should increase either earning capacity or efficiency, creating greater profits to stack in the future. This compounding effect is not always immediate but becomes significant over time. A simple example is using profits from a small business to upgrade tools or systems that reduce workload, which frees capacity to take on more clients, which in turn produces more profits to reinvest. The growth builds in layers rather than isolated leaps.

This process requires clarity on priorities. Redeploying profits without direction can lead to scattered efforts that fail to build momentum. Before committing funds, define what outcome you are optimizing for — greater cash flow, long-term equity, or skill development that unlocks higher earning potential. Clear priorities ensure each reinvestment strengthens your broader strategy instead of creating unrelated projects that compete for time and energy.

Avoiding overextension is equally important. Success often tempts people to scale too quickly, taking on excessive risk or overleveraging in pursuit of rapid growth. Profits should fuel sustainable expansion, not reckless bets. The most enduring wealth builders pace themselves, ensuring each stage is stable before layering on the next. They treat capital as a resource to be respected, knowing that a single misstep can undo years of disciplined stacking.

A common mistake is redeploying profits back into the same venture without considering diminishing returns. While doubling down can be effective, it is wise to assess when diversification provides better long-term stability. Spreading profits into complementary areas — such as converting earned income into investments that generate passive returns — creates resilience. This way, if one income source falters, others continue producing, keeping momentum intact.

Another factor to consider is liquidity. Redeploying everything into long-term assets can leave you cash-poor and unable to respond to new opportunities or unexpected challenges. Maintaining a portion of profits in accessible reserves ensures flexibility. This balance between reinvestment and liquidity evolves as your financial base strengthens, but it should never be ignored entirely.

Over time, stacking and redeploying profits shifts your relationship with money. It moves you from a cycle of earning and spending to a cycle of growth and reinvestment. The focus shifts from how much you make in a single transaction to how effectively each win fuels the next stage of progress. This mindset compounds faster than most realize; small, consistent reinvestments can surpass dramatic one-time gains in their long-term impact.

The ultimate goal is to create a self-sustaining engine — a system where profits continually generate new opportunities and where each layer of growth supports the next. When done correctly, this approach not only builds wealth but also provides a sense of control and clarity. You no longer feel dependent on external circumstances because your financial foundation grows stronger with every cycle, positioning you to act from a place of strength regardless of what challenges or opportunities arise in the future.

Chapter 8: Skill Acquisition and Monetization

The New High-Income Skills

The modern economy rewards a different set of abilities than it did even a decade ago. Where traditional paths emphasized technical degrees or tenure within a single company, today's highest-earning opportunities favor agility, creativity, and the ability to solve problems that cannot easily be automated. These high-income skills are not limited to coding or finance; they span persuasion, analysis, storytelling, and strategy — the very areas where human insight still outperforms machines.

Why Skills Outpace Credentials

Credentials once acted as the primary gatekeeper to high earning potential. A degree from the right university or certification in a specific field almost guaranteed a well-paying career. That advantage has eroded. Information is now widely accessible, and many of the most lucrative industries — tech, online business, digital media — reward demonstrable ability over formal qualifications. Employers and clients increasingly prioritize what you can produce rather than what is printed on a diploma.

This shift opens the door for those willing to learn outside traditional systems. Self-education, mentorship, and hands-on experimentation can elevate someone to expert status in months rather than years. The barrier to entry has lowered, but the bar for performance has risen. Results are the new resume, and those who can deliver tangible outcomes command premium rates.

The Skills That Drive Modern Wealth

Among the most valuable are skills centered on communication and influence. Copywriting, for example, has evolved from simple advertising to a core driver of online commerce. The ability to write words that persuade, inform, and convert directly translates to revenue for businesses. Likewise, public speaking and storytelling have become vital, not only for leaders but also for creators building audiences around personal brands.

Equally powerful are analytical and strategic skills. Digital marketing, data interpretation, and product positioning allow individuals to identify opportunities others miss. Those who can combine creative vision with measurable strategy bridge a gap that most professionals fail to cross, making them indispensable in fast-moving industries.

Technical literacy remains critical, but the focus has shifted from deep specialization to adaptable fluency. Understanding automation tools, AI integration, or the basics of software development provides leverage even if you are not a full-time programmer. These skills allow you to collaborate with specialists, translate complex processes into actionable strategies, and stay ahead in industries that evolve by the year.

Learning High-Income Skills Efficiently

The traditional model of spending years in formal education does not align with the speed of modern opportunity. Instead, skill acquisition now favors concentrated, outcome-driven learning. Online platforms, specialized courses, and project-based practice enable rapid growth. The key is deliberate focus: choosing one or two core skills, applying them in real-world contexts, and building a portfolio of results that demonstrates competence.

High-income skills are not learned once and mastered forever. They evolve alongside technology and consumer behavior. Committing to continuous improvement — staying current with trends, testing new strategies, and refining through feedback — ensures your abilities remain relevant and valuable.

Combining multiple high-income skills creates a multiplier effect. Mastering one valuable skill can generate income, but pairing it with a complementary one increases impact and earning potential dramatically. A digital marketer who also understands persuasive copywriting can design campaigns that not only reach the right audience but also convert at a higher rate. A skilled speaker who understands social media strategy can turn a single talk into a content ecosystem that attracts clients long after the event ends. This synergy transforms isolated abilities into a cohesive personal advantage that is difficult for competitors to replicate.

Positioning yourself in the right markets is just as important as the skills themselves. The same ability can command vastly different rates depending on where it is applied. Copywriting for small businesses may pay modestly, while applying that same skill to high-ticket products or specialized industries like finance or healthcare can be significantly more lucrative. Understanding which markets value your skills most allows you to focus on areas where demand and willingness to pay are highest.

Monetization begins with demonstrating value before expecting reward. Clients and employers often respond better to proof than promises. Building a portfolio — even through unpaid or self-initiated projects at first — provides tangible evidence of capability. These early examples create social proof, making it easier to justify premium pricing later. As credibility grows, referrals and inbound opportunities replace the need for constant outreach.

An often-overlooked element of monetizing high-income skills is personal branding. In a crowded marketplace, visibility and reputation play a pivotal role in attracting opportunities. Sharing insights publicly, documenting your learning journey, and contributing value through content establishes authority long before you make a direct offer. This creates a pull effect where people seek you out rather than you constantly having to chase them.

Scaling income from these skills involves moving beyond direct exchanges of time for money. At first, the goal is mastery and proof of concept, often through freelance work, consulting, or employment. Over time, the focus shifts to leverage — creating products, systems, or intellectual property that generate income without constant direct involvement. Courses, memberships, templates, and licensing are examples of how individuals turn active skills into semi-passive revenue streams, multiplying earning potential without sacrificing quality.

The discipline required to maintain this growth cannot be overstated. High-income skills can open doors quickly, but without ongoing refinement they can just as quickly become outdated. Industries change, algorithms shift, and consumer preferences evolve. Committing to lifelong learning, regularly assessing your positioning, and reinvesting part of your earnings into skill development ensures you remain competitive in the long run.

The true power of these skills lies not only in the financial outcomes but also in the autonomy they create. Being able to generate value independent of traditional employment structures offers freedom to choose projects, set terms, and design a lifestyle aligned with personal priorities. That autonomy is the hallmark of modern wealth — the ability to control your time, direct your energy toward meaningful work, and continuously evolve as opportunities expand.

Compounding Skill Stacks

Skill acquisition is often approached in isolation. People learn one ability, apply it, and then move on to another. While this can be effective in the short term, it misses the exponential power of stacking skills deliberately. A skill stack is not just a list of unrelated abilities; it is a carefully chosen combination that multiplies effectiveness when combined. This approach creates unique value, positioning you far beyond competitors who rely on singular expertise.

The Mechanics of a Skill Stack

Every skill has standalone value, but when combined with others it can unlock opportunities that would otherwise remain inaccessible. For example, someone skilled in financial analysis may earn a solid income. Pairing that skill with persuasive communication can transform them into a sought-after advisor or consultant who not only understands the numbers but can also influence decisions at the highest levels. Each additional skill in the stack expands the range of problems you can solve and the level of value you can provide.

Skill stacks compound because they are rare. Many people can write, but few can write persuasively about complex technical topics. Many people can analyze data, but few can communicate those insights in ways that drive business action. The scarcity created by combining abilities makes you difficult to replace and allows you to command higher rates or salaries.

Choosing Skills That Complement Each Other

Not all skills combine well. The key is choosing abilities that naturally enhance one another rather than pulling you in conflicting directions. Start with a core competency — something you are already good at or interested in mastering — and identify adjacent skills that elevate it. For example, a marketer might add copywriting, data analysis, and behavioral psychology to create a comprehensive understanding of how to attract and convert customers. A product designer could pair design thinking with storytelling and negotiation to navigate both creative and business dimensions.

Selecting skills with overlapping applications ensures each new ability strengthens the previous ones rather than competing for your focus. Over time, this creates a network effect: every new skill reinforces the entire stack, making you progressively more versatile and valuable.

Building in Layers

Skill stacking works best when built in deliberate layers rather than all at once. Attempting to learn several complex abilities simultaneously leads to shallow understanding and burnout. Instead, focus on developing one skill to competence, then add another that complements it, applying both together in real projects. This layering approach ensures practical integration rather than theoretical knowledge.

Each layer builds momentum. As your first skills begin to generate opportunities, you can reinvest time, energy, and sometimes profits into acquiring the next skill. This creates a self-reinforcing cycle where learning fuels income, which in turn funds deeper learning. Over time, your career trajectory shifts from linear to exponential growth.

High-leverage combinations emerge when a skill from one domain unlocks unique applications in another. A person who understands negotiation and combines it with deep product knowledge can close deals others cannot. A content creator who also studies data analytics can tailor messages based on real-time feedback, leading to higher engagement and faster growth. This cross-pollination is what gives skill stacks their compounding effect: value increases not in a straight line but in accelerating curves as each ability amplifies the others.

Applying stacks in real-world scenarios requires consistent experimentation. Theory alone does not reveal which combinations resonate most with the market. Offering your skills in small projects, freelance work, or even personal ventures provides the feedback needed to refine your positioning. Over time, you will notice patterns — certain abilities create leverage more often than others, while some may be less impactful than anticipated. Adjusting based on these insights ensures your stack evolves with actual demand rather than abstract assumptions.

The reputation you build around your stack becomes a powerful asset. As people associate you with a rare mix of abilities, opportunities begin to find you rather than the other way around. This shift moves you from chasing prospects to attracting them, allowing you to focus on higher-level opportunities. Protecting and nurturing this reputation is essential; a single broken promise or inconsistent delivery can damage years of credibility. Integrity, consistency, and visible results are what transform a skill stack from potential into lasting influence.

Over time, stacking skills also reduces vulnerability to economic shifts. Industries rise and fall, but a diverse set of complementary abilities allows you to pivot without starting over. When one market slows, you can reframe your skills to serve another. This adaptability not only protects income but often opens unexpected doors to higher-paying opportunities. It is this flexibility that distinguishes those who merely survive disruption from those who thrive during it.

As your stack matures, the compounding becomes evident in more than just financial outcomes. Confidence grows as you realize you can solve problems others cannot. Creativity flourishes because you draw insights from multiple fields rather than a single perspective. This multidisciplinary view enables innovation, often leading to breakthroughs that specialists overlook. The result is a personal moat — a competitive advantage so unique that imitation becomes difficult, even for those willing to invest heavily.

The ultimate aim of compounding skill stacks is not simply to earn more but to create leverage over your time and choices. By offering rare value, you gain negotiating power, whether in employment, entrepreneurship, or partnerships. You can choose projects that align with your goals rather than scrambling for whatever is available. Over the long term, this freedom becomes the most valuable dividend your skill stack provides — a life built on intentional growth, not reactive survival.

Turning Skills Into Leverage

Acquiring high-income skills is powerful, but their true potential is unlocked when those skills are used as leverage. Leverage means that the results of your effort are amplified, allowing you to achieve far more than you could through raw labor alone. It is the difference between someone who trades hours for income and someone who creates value that continues to generate returns even when they are not actively working. Skills by themselves provide opportunity; leverage transforms that opportunity into exponential growth.

Understanding the Nature of Leverage

Leverage allows you to multiply the impact of your abilities without multiplying your workload. A skilled writer can earn a living producing individual pieces of content for clients, but when that same writer creates an email sequence that sells a product on autopilot or builds a digital course consumed by thousands, the same skill produces far greater results. The writer's words remain the same, but their reach and earning potential expand dramatically because they are no longer bound by direct time-to-income exchange.

There are several forms of leverage that can transform skills into scalable assets. Tools and technology extend what one person can accomplish — automation, AI, and software systems reduce repetitive work and allow focus on higher-level strategy. Capital acts as leverage by funding initiatives that multiply returns, whether through advertising, product development, or investments. Networks provide another layer of leverage, as each connection can open doors to opportunities and audiences far beyond what individual effort could achieve.

From Practitioner to Builder

The shift begins when you stop viewing your skills purely as services to sell and start seeing them as building blocks for systems and assets. Instead of thinking, "How do I earn with this skill?" the better question is, "How do I design a system that uses this skill to create ongoing value?" This mindset is what differentiates a practitioner from a builder.

For example, a digital marketer can run campaigns for individual clients indefinitely, earning respectable income but remaining limited by time. If that same marketer builds their own brand, develops templates, or creates a proprietary framework that others can license or learn from, they move from practitioner to builder. The work they have already done compounds, generating income beyond the immediate contract.

The Role of Intellectual Property

One of the most effective ways to create leverage is through intellectual property. Knowledge packaged into products — books, courses, software, or frameworks — allows you to monetize expertise repeatedly without recreating it each time. Once created, these assets can be distributed at scale, reaching audiences globally without proportional increases in effort. This is why so many modern entrepreneurs focus on building digital products or codifying their methods into repeatable systems.

Even in traditional roles, creating intellectual property sets you apart. A consultant who develops a unique methodology can license it to multiple firms. A designer who builds a signature style or toolkit can sell it to peers and clients alike. By turning knowledge into a tangible asset, you free yourself from purely transactional work and position yourself for exponential growth.

Identifying opportunities for leverage begins with examining where your skills produce disproportionate results. Look for moments where a single action creates recurring value or where expertise allows you to solve problems others cannot. These areas often indicate potential for systems or assets that scale beyond your personal involvement. For instance, if a strategy you use consistently drives measurable results for clients, packaging that strategy into a framework or tool transforms it into something replicable and monetizable.

Integrating multiple forms of leverage magnifies the effect even further. Combining intellectual property with networks and technology, for example, creates exponential reach. A coach who develops a proven method can package it into an online course, automate delivery through digital platforms, and amplify distribution through strategic partnerships or affiliates. Each layer of leverage builds on the others, multiplying impact without equivalent increases in effort.

Transitioning from individual contributor to architect requires a shift in how you allocate time and resources. Instead of focusing solely on performing the skill, begin investing in building the infrastructure around it. This might mean documenting processes, training others, or developing scalable assets. At first, this can feel slower than direct execution, but it creates a foundation that eventually allows growth to accelerate without your constant input.

One challenge in this transition is letting go of the belief that only you can deliver quality. Many high performers resist delegating or systemizing because they fear losing control. In reality, leverage does not diminish quality when done intentionally; it preserves it by creating consistent frameworks others can follow. The best systems enhance your expertise rather than dilute it, allowing you to operate at a higher level while still delivering exceptional results.

Monetizing leveraged skills often requires reframing how you present your value. Clients or audiences may be accustomed to paying for your time, not your systems. Demonstrating the outcomes your approach delivers, rather than the hours it requires, shifts perception from cost to investment. This is where positioning and branding play a key role — the more your expertise is perceived as unique and outcome-driven, the easier it becomes to command premium rates for assets rather than labor.

Over time, leveraging skills creates optionality. You gain the freedom to choose projects based on alignment rather than necessity because your income is no longer tied solely to active work. This flexibility allows greater creativity, more selective opportunities, and the ability to pivot into new ventures without sacrificing financial stability. It is this combination of freedom and growth that defines true leverage — a state where your skills not only earn but compound, building a foundation that continues to expand long after the initial effort has been invested.

Chapter 9: The Invisible Forces of Money (Energy + Psychology)

Money as Energy, Not Paper

Most people grow up seeing money as something physical, even if they rarely touch cash anymore. It is treated as pieces of paper or numbers on a screen, valuable because society agrees it is valuable. But this view is incomplete. To truly master wealth, you need to understand money as energy — a flow of value that moves through systems, relationships, and opportunities. This perspective changes how you earn, spend, and invest. It also removes the emotional weight that often causes fear or shame around finances.

The Flow of Money

When seen as energy, money is not static. It flows between people and entities, constantly moving toward value and away from waste. Businesses exchange products or services for it, investors move it into assets, and individuals trade it for convenience or experiences. This movement reveals something important: money follows attention and intention. Where you focus energy in your life, money tends to flow, because attention drives creation and creation drives value.

This is why people who obsess over lack often find themselves stuck in cycles of scarcity. Their energy is spent worrying rather than building. Conversely, those who approach money as a tool for expansion — focusing on opportunities, relationships, and growth — tend to attract more of it. It is not mystical; it is psychological and practical. Your decisions shape your outcomes, and decisions are influenced by how you perceive money.

Money as Stored Potential

Another way to view money-as-energy is to see it as stored potential. When you have savings, investments, or even available credit, you hold the potential to direct that energy into something greater. That potential can be squandered on fleeting comforts or invested in assets, skills, or ventures that multiply. The difference lies not in the amount of money itself, but in the wisdom of how it is directed.

This idea reframes saving and investing. Saving is not about hoarding paper; it is about storing energy until the right opportunity arises. Investing is not just about returns; it is about directing energy toward growth. Even spending, when intentional, can be a form of energy exchange — trading resources for experiences, knowledge, or tools that improve your life and expand future potential.

Emotional Detachment and Empowerment

Viewing money as energy also helps remove unhealthy emotional attachment. Many people tie their self-worth to their bank balance, feeling secure when it rises and anxious when it falls. This leads to reactive choices: clinging to money out of fear or chasing quick wins to ease insecurity. By seeing money as neutral energy — neither good nor bad, simply a resource — you gain emotional clarity. You stop judging yourself for past mistakes and start making decisions from a place of purpose rather than panic.

Detachment does not mean indifference. It means approaching money with calm focus. You respect its power without fearing it, and you value it without worshiping it. This balanced mindset allows clearer thinking, better planning, and ultimately, greater growth.

When you begin treating money as energy, the focus shifts from accumulation to flow. The goal is no longer to simply gather as much as possible but to ensure that what flows into your life is directed purposefully and what flows out returns to you in greater form. This is the foundation of building wealth that grows rather than stagnates. Money held without purpose loses power; money circulated with intention compounds in both tangible and intangible ways.

Alignment with this flow begins by clarifying what you value. If energy follows intention, then unclear intentions create scattered results. Without clarity, it is easy to fall into patterns of reaction, spending impulsively or investing without strategy. But when you define what money is meant to support — whether freedom, impact, or security — every decision gains context. Choices about saving, spending, and earning become part of a larger system rather than isolated transactions.

Directing energy effectively also means removing leaks. Just as physical energy is drained by habits that harm the body, financial energy is drained by unconscious spending, high-interest debt, and obligations that do not align with priorities. Identifying and closing these leaks creates immediate breathing room. The freed energy can then be redirected toward assets, skills, or experiences that produce returns rather than diminishing resources. Circulation is key. Money that sits idle loses momentum, especially in times of inflation or missed opportunity. Yet circulation must be deliberate. There is a difference between spending recklessly and investing strategically. Even purchases that appear like spending — such as health, education, or tools — can be investments if they increase your capacity to create value in the future. The question to ask is not simply "What does this cost?" but "What does this return over time?"

A powerful effect of adopting this mindset is how it influences relationships with others. When you view money as energy, transactions shift from being purely financial to being exchanges of value. This applies in business partnerships, sales, or even personal interactions. When both parties bring value to the table, energy flows in a way that sustains growth rather than draining it. This is why collaboration often accelerates wealth faster than solitary effort — combined energy multiplies potential rather than merely adding to it.

Over time, living by this principle fosters resilience. Economic downturns or unexpected expenses become less destabilizing because you no longer see them as permanent losses of paper but as shifts in energy that can be redirected. You understand that value can always be created, that energy can be regenerated, and that wealth is less about static numbers than about your ability to channel flow in any circumstance.

Ultimately, this perspective invites a deeper form of freedom. Money is no longer a source of anxiety or endless pursuit; it becomes a resource you manage with clarity and confidence. By aligning energy with intention, you create systems where wealth supports your life rather than dictates it. This shift not only transforms how you handle finances but also how you approach opportunity, risk, and the impact you aim to leave behind.

The Role of Identity and Self-Worth

The results you create with money are deeply tied to how you see yourself. People rarely outperform the identity they hold. Someone who unconsciously believes they are bad with money will sabotage opportunities, dismiss possibilities, or cling to scarcity even when new income appears. Conversely, a person who views themselves as capable of building and managing wealth approaches decisions with clarity and confidence, often achieving results that seem out of reach to others with similar resources.

Identity as a Financial Thermostat

Identity functions like a thermostat for your financial life. No matter how much external success you achieve, you tend to return to what feels familiar internally. This is why sudden windfalls often vanish and why long-term wealth is most often built by those whose internal beliefs rise in alignment with their external results. If you secretly believe you are undeserving of abundance, you will find ways to bring yourself back down to a level that matches that belief, whether through overspending, procrastination, or neglecting opportunities.

This concept works in the opposite direction as well. If your self-worth is high but your current circumstances are limited, you naturally seek ways to rise to the level of your inner expectations. You pursue opportunities others ignore, invest in yourself, and treat setbacks as temporary rather than defining. Over time, your external world begins to reflect your internal standard.

The Stories We Carry

Our financial identity is shaped by stories we inherit and internalize. Many people grow up hearing phrases like "money doesn't grow on trees," "rich people are greedy," or "we can't afford that." These messages, repeated over years, imprint a worldview where money is scarce, hard to obtain, or morally questionable. Without examining these beliefs, they quietly dictate behavior well into adulthood. Even ambitious individuals can unknowingly limit themselves by operating from inherited narratives that no longer serve them.

Challenging these stories begins with awareness. By identifying the messages you absorbed about money and questioning their truth, you create space to rewrite them. Were those beliefs accurate, or were they shaped by the circumstances of the people who passed them down? Does holding onto them still serve your goals, or are they keeping you in cycles you are ready to outgrow?

Self-Worth and Earning Capacity

There is a direct link between self-worth and earning potential. People who undervalue themselves often undercharge for their work, avoid negotiating, or hesitate to pursue higher-paying opportunities because they fear rejection. Those with stronger self-worth view their contributions objectively and advocate for fair compensation. This difference compounds over time — two people with similar skills can experience vastly different financial trajectories simply because one believes they deserve more and acts accordingly.

This is not about arrogance or entitlement; it is about accurately recognizing the value you provide. When you see yourself as someone who creates meaningful impact, you naturally make decisions that align with that identity, from how you market your skills to how you invest in your own development.

Shifting financial identity starts with conscious alignment between beliefs, language, and daily actions. If you continue to speak and act as if you are limited, even small opportunities will feel out of reach. Begin by examining how you describe yourself and your relationship with money. Do you use phrases like "I'm terrible with finances" or "I can't afford that"? Subtle language patterns reinforce identity. Reframing those statements into ones that affirm growth — such as "I'm learning to manage my money well" or "I'm choosing how to allocate my resources" — creates a shift that seems small but compounds over time.

Beliefs must be reinforced through consistent action. Identity is strengthened every time you follow through on choices aligned with your desired self-concept. For example, if you want to see yourself as someone who invests wisely, start by directing even a small amount toward learning and practicing those skills. Each act becomes evidence that supports the new identity. Over weeks and months, these choices shift self-perception from aspiration to truth.

Environment plays a powerful role in this process. Surrounding yourself with people who normalize higher standards raises your own. If you spend most of your time around individuals who view wealth as unattainable or who reinforce scarcity, it becomes harder to sustain new beliefs. Conversely, exposure to those who think abundantly and act strategically helps rewire what feels possible. This does not mean abandoning old relationships but intentionally seeking influences that expand rather than contract your vision.

A practical tool for elevating self-worth is tracking value created rather than only income earned. When you measure the positive impact of your work — results for clients, problems solved, innovations brought forward — you begin to see evidence of worth that may not yet be fully reflected in your bank account. This awareness fuels the confidence to negotiate better terms, pursue new markets, or invest in personal growth.

Identity work also requires patience. Deeply ingrained beliefs rarely vanish overnight. There may be moments where old patterns resurface, especially during stress or setbacks. Rather than treating these as failures, view them as signals pointing to areas that still need reinforcement. Consistent reflection, journaling, or coaching can help integrate new beliefs until they become second nature.

The long-term reward of aligning self-worth with financial potential is stability. Instead of being swayed by external circumstances, your internal standard anchors you. Sudden gains do not feel overwhelming because you are prepared to manage them, and temporary losses do not shatter you because you trust your ability to recover. Money becomes a tool rather than a measure of personal value, freeing you to make clearer decisions and pursue opportunities that align with purpose, not fear.

When your identity rises, your actions follow. Opportunities you once overlooked become visible, conversations you once avoided become natural, and strategies you once doubted become achievable. Over time, this alignment creates a compounding effect: self-worth fuels better choices, better choices create better results, and those results reinforce self-worth. This cycle becomes the foundation for lasting wealth and the confidence to sustain it.

Aligning Energy with Action

Lasting wealth is created when internal alignment meets external execution. Many people work hard yet feel drained, scattered, or stuck because their actions are out of sync with their energy. They follow strategies that look good on paper but ignore what fuels or depletes them. Aligning energy with action is about closing that gap — ensuring that how you show up daily matches the direction you want your life and finances to move toward.

The Cost of Misalignment

When actions are misaligned with energy, progress feels forced. You might take on projects that pay well but leave you uninspired, or work tirelessly toward goals that no longer resonate. Over time, this creates burnout, resentment, and inconsistent results. It also affects decision-making: exhaustion narrows perspective, leading to short-term fixes instead of long-term solutions. This cycle is why some people achieve financial milestones yet feel unfulfilled — they are chasing outcomes disconnected from who they are becoming.

The reverse is equally challenging. People with strong vision and high aspirations often struggle when they lack consistent action to ground that energy. Ideas remain unexecuted, opportunities pass by, and confidence erodes. Without discipline, inspiration becomes frustration. The key is finding the balance where energy fuels action and action reinforces energy, creating a feedback loop of momentum.

Understanding Personal Energy Patterns

Aligning energy begins with awareness. Energy is not constant; it fluctuates daily and across seasons of life. Some individuals are naturally most productive in the morning, while others thrive later in the day. Certain tasks energize — creative problem-solving, building relationships, learning new skills — while others drain, such as administrative work or repetitive routines. By mapping your personal energy patterns, you can schedule high-impact actions during peak states and reserve low-energy periods for tasks that require less creativity or focus.

This awareness also applies to broader life phases. There are times when building aggressively aligns with your energy — launching a business, scaling income, or taking calculated risks. Other seasons require consolidation and recovery — paying down debt, stabilizing systems, or protecting mental bandwidth. Recognizing which phase you are in prevents unnecessary resistance and helps you design actions that fit current capacity without losing sight of the larger vision.

Values as a Source of Energy

Energy is sustained when actions align with values. If freedom, creativity, or contribution are core drivers for you, work that violates those values will quickly drain motivation, no matter the financial reward. Clarifying personal values provides a compass for decision-making. It helps you choose opportunities that amplify energy rather than deplete it and ensures that financial goals are not pursued at the expense of well-being.

Values-driven alignment also improves consistency. Motivation rooted in external pressure fades quickly; motivation rooted in personal meaning endures. When you know why something matters beyond money alone, you approach challenges with greater resilience. This internal fuel makes it easier to stay committed through setbacks and to recognize which sacrifices are worth making and which are not.

Practical alignment starts with designing routines that prioritize energy first, not tasks. Instead of cramming as much activity as possible into a day, structure it around your highest-value actions during your peak energetic windows. This might mean reserving mornings for creative or strategic work and afternoons for administrative tasks or meetings. Protecting these windows builds consistency and prevents the frustration of expending prime energy on low-impact work.

A second layer of alignment is creating rituals that prepare you to act. Small habits — setting intentions before starting work, reviewing priorities the night before, or using brief resets between tasks — signal your mind and body to focus. Over time, these rituals reduce friction and make high-quality action automatic rather than something you need to force through willpower alone. Consistency here compounds just as financial investments do: small gains build momentum that grows over weeks and months.

Guarding against energy leaks is equally important. Misaligned commitments, unclear boundaries, and constant digital distractions quietly drain focus and leave little left for meaningful work. Regularly auditing your schedule and obligations helps identify where energy is being lost without producing value. Eliminating or delegating even one unnecessary task can free mental bandwidth to focus on actions that move you closer to your goals.

The bridge between energy and action is prioritization. Without clear priorities, energy is scattered across competing demands, and even strong effort yields minimal results. Identifying the few actions that create the greatest impact — what some call the vital few — ensures your best energy fuels the most meaningful outcomes. This focus prevents burnout because progress becomes visible, reinforcing motivation and signaling that your actions matter.

Sustaining alignment over the long term requires flexibility. Energy and priorities shift as life evolves, and systems must adapt. Building regular checkpoints into your routine, such as weekly reviews or quarterly resets, allows you to evaluate what is working and what needs adjustment. These reviews prevent drift, ensuring that actions remain connected to your current goals and values rather than outdated assumptions about what success should look like.

An often-overlooked aspect of alignment is recovery. Energy is renewable, but only if replenished. Strategic rest — quality sleep, movement, time in nature, and meaningful connection — is not indulgence but fuel for sustained performance. Those who neglect recovery eventually hit ceilings, mistaking exhaustion for lack of ability rather than mismanagement of energy. By honoring rest as part of the wealth-building process, you preserve the clarity and resilience required to make sound financial decisions.

Ultimately, aligning energy with action creates a state of flow where momentum feels natural rather than forced. Work becomes more intentional, decisions clearer, and progress steadier. This harmony between inner state and outward behavior accelerates results while reducing the stress and burnout that derail so many on the path to financial independence. It transforms wealth-building from a constant uphill battle into a sustainable rhythm — one where every step forward strengthens both the outcome and the person creating it.

Chapter 10: Building Unfair Advantages

Positioning Yourself Where Others Can't Compete

In every industry, there are crowded spaces where everyone fights for attention and undervalued spaces where opportunity thrives. The people who achieve outsized success rarely do so by competing in the obvious arenas. Instead, they position themselves where competition is weak or irrelevant, creating advantages that others cannot easily copy. This kind of positioning is less about working harder and more about playing a different game entirely.

The Principle of Unique Positioning

Unique positioning begins with understanding that most markets reward differentiation, not sameness. Competing on price or sheer effort places you in a race to the bottom. By contrast, competing on perspective, skill combinations, or unique insight creates separation. This separation allows you to command higher value and attract opportunities without constant struggle. When you occupy a position others cannot easily replicate, you stop chasing work and start drawing it to you.

Leveraging Personal Advantages

Every individual has inherent advantages, though most overlook them. These advantages may come from life experience, specialized knowledge, or an unusual combination of skills. Someone with a background in both psychology and marketing, for example, can craft campaigns that resonate at a deeper level than marketers focused solely on data. Similarly, a person who understands finance and storytelling can explain complex concepts in ways that appeal to investors and customers alike. The key is not trying to outdo others at their strengths but identifying intersections where your unique combination stands alone.

This approach requires deep self-awareness. Many people undervalue what feels normal to them, assuming everyone shares their abilities or insights. They fail to recognize that what is easy for them might be difficult for others and therefore valuable. Taking inventory of skills, experiences, and perspectives that differentiate you is a crucial first step in discovering where competition thins out.

Choosing the Right Playing Field

Even exceptional skills can lose power in the wrong environment. Positioning yourself where others cannot compete means deliberately selecting markets, clients, or opportunities where your advantages matter most. This is why some people thrive after switching industries or focusing on niches ignored by bigger players. In a crowded mainstream market, differentiation is harder to communicate. In a specialized space, even modest expertise can make you indispensable.

The right positioning also considers timing. Emerging trends often create windows of opportunity where few are paying attention. Those who recognize and act early can establish themselves as authorities before the space becomes crowded. This pattern is visible in technology, media, and finance, where early adopters often appear "lucky" but are actually leveraging foresight.

Building Barriers to Imitation

A powerful position is one that others struggle to copy. This is achieved not by secrecy but by depth and integration. When your value comes from layers of expertise, reputation, and relationships, imitation becomes difficult. Competitors may replicate surface tactics but cannot easily match the credibility or trust built over years of consistent work. This depth turns positioning into a durable advantage, one that compounds as time passes.

Strengthening a unique position begins with clarity. If you cannot articulate what sets you apart, neither can the people you want to reach. Defining this requires more than a clever slogan; it means identifying the exact problems you solve, the distinct perspective you bring, and why those elements matter to the people you serve. The clearer and more specific this message becomes, the easier it is for others to recognize your value immediately.

Communicating this position consistently is what transforms it from an idea into a reputation. Repetition across different touchpoints — how you write, speak, network, and present your work — reinforces the perception of authority. Over time, this reputation begins to precede you. Opportunities come not because you chase them but because your name is already associated with certain results or qualities. This is where positioning shifts from active effort to compounding advantage.

Evolving the position is equally important. Markets change, competitors adapt, and what is rare today may become common tomorrow. Staying ahead requires continual refinement of your unique edge. This may mean adding new skills, shifting focus to an emerging trend, or deepening expertise in a way others are unwilling to invest in. Rather than defending a static position, you treat your uniqueness as a living system that grows more robust over time.

Relationships form a critical part of this evolution. Positioning is amplified by who knows and trusts you, not just what you know. Strategic alliances, mentorships, and collaborations expand your reach and embed you deeper into networks that competitors cannot easily access. These relationships also provide insight into shifts within your field, allowing you to adapt before others even notice the change.

Another layer of strength comes from building proof into everything you do. Testimonials, case studies, and demonstrable results create undeniable evidence of value. While others rely on claims, you rely on outcomes. This credibility forms a barrier against competition because trust is hard to duplicate. Even if someone matches your technical ability, they cannot replicate the history of results you have built.

Ultimately, positioning where others cannot compete frees you from the exhausting cycle of comparison. Instead of measuring progress against peers, you measure against your own evolving standard. The focus shifts from outperforming others to refining what only you can deliver. This is where true leverage emerges — not by being slightly better in the same arena, but by playing a game that few others even see, let alone know how to win.

Information Arbitrage

Opportunities often hide in plain sight, not because they are invisible, but because most people do not recognize their value. Information arbitrage is the practice of identifying knowledge that is undervalued or overlooked in one context and applying it in another where it carries greater significance. It is not about insider secrets or unethical shortcuts. It is about seeing patterns others miss, connecting dots others ignore, and acting on insights before they become obvious.

The Edge Created by Uneven Knowledge

Information has never been more abundant, yet valuable insight remains rare. Most people drown in data without knowing how to filter, interpret, or apply it. This creates a gap between what is available and what is actionable. Those who bridge this gap gain an edge. They can identify trends earlier, spot inefficiencies in systems, and capitalize on opportunities while others are still catching up.

This edge does not come from consuming more information but from consuming differently. Where most chase headlines and surface-level summaries, skilled practitioners go deeper. They study original sources, analyze overlooked details, and extract principles that remain useful long after trends shift. In this way, they transform noise into clarity and clarity into leverage.

Recognizing Hidden Value

The heart of information arbitrage lies in recognizing when knowledge is mispriced. This could be an emerging technology understood by only a small group, a strategy proven in one industry but ignored in another, or a historical lesson that applies to modern challenges. When you identify something others underestimate, you gain the ability to act decisively while the window of opportunity is still open.

Timing plays a crucial role. Valuable information eventually spreads, and once widely known, its advantage diminishes. The goal is not to hoard knowledge but to position yourself early enough to benefit from it before the market fully adjusts. This requires vigilance — staying curious, questioning assumptions, and observing patterns long before they appear in mainstream conversation.

Building a System for Insight

Relying on chance discovery is not sustainable. To consistently find mispriced information, you need a deliberate system. This begins with selecting key areas of focus rather than trying to track everything. Depth in a few domains yields far more opportunities than shallow awareness of many. Once focus areas are chosen, structure how you gather and analyze information. Create a rhythm for reviewing sources, testing ideas, and capturing insights in ways that make them easy to apply.

Equally important is cross-pollination between fields. Breakthroughs often occur at the intersections of disciplines, where few people bother to look. A technique common in software engineering might revolutionize marketing. A behavioral insight from psychology could transform investment strategies. By connecting unrelated areas, you uncover value invisible to specialists trapped in silos.

Turning insights into results begins with testing. Not every overlooked piece of information leads to opportunity, and acting blindly can waste resources. The key is applying small-scale experiments to validate assumptions before scaling. This might involve trying a new marketing approach on a single product line, investing a modest sum in an under-the-radar asset, or running a pilot project that leverages knowledge borrowed from another field. Rapid testing turns theory into measurable outcomes and reveals whether the arbitrage is real or imagined.

Monetization happens when the insight moves from personal advantage to systematic use. Once proven, a discovery can become part of a repeatable process: an investment framework, a unique service offering, or a product designed around an unmet need. Those who treat each insight as part of a larger system build compounding advantage; each successful discovery adds to a growing base of tools and knowledge that makes finding the next opportunity easier.

Assessing which opportunities to pursue requires understanding both potential upside and execution difficulty. Some information gaps offer large rewards but demand significant resources or specialized skills to exploit. Others may yield smaller but consistent advantages that compound over time. Developing criteria for evaluation — potential return, time horizon, scalability, and personal alignment — ensures focus on insights that truly move the needle rather than chasing distractions.

Ethics remain central to sustainable arbitrage. Exploiting confidential information or misleading others for gain may yield short-term wins but destroys trust and reputation, which are essential for long-term success. The strongest opportunities come from public or widely available information that others fail to see, not from secrecy or manipulation. This approach positions you as a trusted authority rather than a questionable opportunist, attracting partnerships and referrals that expand reach even further.

As information becomes more abundant, the ability to filter and synthesize becomes a defining skill. While others grow overwhelmed by the noise, those who develop frameworks for spotting patterns and undervalued insights gain a permanent edge. They are not simply consuming data; they are shaping meaning from it, anticipating shifts before they happen, and aligning their actions to capitalize on those shifts at the right moment.

Over time, practicing information arbitrage transforms how you view the world. Markets, careers, and opportunities stop appearing random and start revealing structure. Patterns emerge where others see chaos. You begin to trust your ability to find hidden value in plain sight, to move confidently while others hesitate, and to create advantages that cannot be bought but must be earned through perception and discipline. This mindset, once internalized, becomes one of the most powerful levers for building lasting wealth and independence.

Systems Over Hustle

Many people believe that working harder is the answer to achieving financial freedom. The hustle culture glorifies long hours, relentless effort, and sacrificing rest for progress. While discipline and hard work have value, relying solely on hustle creates diminishing returns. There is a limit to how many hours you can work and how much energy you can expend before burnout sets in. True scalability comes not from doing more yourself, but from building systems that multiply effort without requiring constant personal input.

The Trap of Endless Effort

Hustle feels productive because it creates immediate results. Completing tasks, answering messages, and constantly staying busy provides a sense of momentum. However, busyness does not always equal progress. Without systems, you are stuck in reactive cycles — chasing opportunities rather than creating them, solving problems repeatedly instead of preventing them. This reactive state leads to exhaustion and stagnation, as growth depends entirely on your ability to work harder rather than smarter.

Over time, this approach can also limit earning potential. If your income is tied only to your personal output, there is a ceiling you cannot break. When you stop working, results stop coming. The goal is to escape this ceiling by building processes that function independently of your constant attention.

Why Systems Create Leverage

Systems transform effort into consistent results. A system is simply a repeatable process that delivers predictable outcomes. It might be a workflow for managing clients, an automated marketing funnel, or a method for reinvesting profits systematically rather than impulsively. Once created, these systems free you from reinventing solutions each time a challenge arises. They save energy, reduce mistakes, and allow focus on higher-value decisions rather than repetitive tasks.

The most powerful systems are those that scale. An automated sales process can serve thousands of customers without extra effort. A documented procedure can enable a team to perform at a high level without constant supervision. By front-loading the work of building systems, you create compounding benefits: more output, fewer errors, and greater consistency over time.

The Shift From Operator to Architect

Moving from hustle to systems requires a mindset shift. Operators focus on tasks; architects focus on structures. As an operator, your question is, "How do I get this done today?" As an architect, your question is, "How do I design a process so this gets done every time without me?" This shift allows you to step back and see the bigger picture — identifying bottlenecks, anticipating future challenges, and designing solutions that endure.

Making this transition can feel uncomfortable at first. Building systems often requires slowing down temporarily to analyze workflows and document processes. It may feel less urgent than pushing through another long day of work. But this short-term slowdown creates long-term speed. Once in place, systems allow you to do more with less stress and open the path to scaling income and impact far beyond what hustle alone could achieve.

Identifying where systems will create the most impact begins with spotting patterns. Repetitive tasks, recurring decisions, and common problems are clear indicators. If something happens more than twice, it likely deserves a system. Start small by documenting the steps you take, then refine them to remove unnecessary complexity. This creates clarity not just for you but for anyone you might eventually delegate to. Clarity is the foundation of scalability.

Designing effective systems means balancing structure with flexibility. A rigid system may collapse when conditions change, while a vague one fails to deliver consistent results. The goal is to create frameworks that standardize key actions while leaving room for adaptation. For example, a content creation system might outline research, drafting, and publishing steps but still allow creative freedom in tone and style. Flexibility ensures the system remains useful as your business or career evolves.

Technology can dramatically enhance this process. Automation tools handle tasks like scheduling, reminders, or customer follow-ups with minimal effort, freeing mental bandwidth for higher-level thinking. However, technology should serve the system, not define it. Automating a flawed process simply multiplies inefficiency. Establish the workflow manually first, confirm it works, then use tools to scale it.

The greatest benefit of systems is not only efficiency but resilience. When you are no longer the bottleneck, opportunities can expand without overwhelming you. A single absence or unexpected challenge will not derail progress because the structure supports continuity. This resilience also makes it easier to pursue new ventures; once a system runs reliably, you can shift energy toward innovation rather than maintenance.

Maintaining systems is as important as building them. Circumstances change, markets shift, and processes that once worked may become outdated. Regular reviews ensure that your systems remain aligned with current goals and opportunities. Treat them as living frameworks — improve them incrementally rather than overhauling them reactively. Small adjustments keep them effective without causing disruption.

Over time, adopting a systems-first approach fundamentally changes your relationship with work. Progress no longer depends on constant hustle or sacrifice. You begin to measure success not by how busy you are but by how seamlessly results occur without your direct involvement. This shift opens space for strategy, creativity, and rest, which in turn fuel even greater performance.

The compounding effect of systems is profound. One well-built process can save hours every week, freeing time to design the next improvement. Each layer of efficiency multiplies the others, eventually creating momentum that feels effortless compared to the grind of endless hustle. This is how sustainable wealth and freedom are built — through thoughtful structures that outlast the energy of any single day.

Chapter 11: The New Rules of Financial Freedom

Designing Autonomy, Not Retirement
For decades, the idea of retirement has been framed as the ultimate financial goal: work hard for forty years, save diligently, and eventually stop working altogether. This model assumes that freedom comes only at the end of life, after sacrificing prime years to a job that often feels more like obligation than choice. But the landscape of work and wealth has changed. True freedom is no longer about escaping work entirely; it is about creating autonomy — the ability to decide how, when, and where you work long before traditional retirement age.

Rethinking the End Goal
The traditional retirement model is rooted in scarcity. It assumes that work is something to be endured, not enjoyed, and that the payoff for decades of sacrifice is the chance to finally rest. Yet many people who reach retirement struggle with purpose once the structure of work disappears. Others find that financial markets, inflation, or health challenges force them back into the workforce anyway. This outdated framework fails to account for a deeper human need: the desire to live with choice and meaning throughout life, not just at its end.

Autonomy reframes the objective. It is not about quitting work but about reshaping it so that it supports your desired lifestyle. With autonomy, you choose projects that interest you, set your schedule, and retain control over your time. Work becomes a vehicle for fulfillment and growth rather than a drain on energy. The focus shifts from an eventual finish line to a series of intentional choices that create freedom now.

Building Life Around Flexibility
Designing for autonomy starts with clarity on what freedom means to you. For some, it is location independence — the ability to travel while maintaining income. For others, it is flexible hours to prioritize family or creative pursuits. Without this clarity, it is easy to chase generic milestones,

such as a specific net worth, only to discover they do not deliver the lifestyle you envisioned.

Once defined, autonomy is built by aligning income, systems, and personal values. This often involves diversifying income streams so that no single source dictates your schedule. Side ventures, digital products, investments, or consultancy work can complement primary income, providing resilience and options. Flexibility grows as you reduce dependency on any single employer, client, or market condition.

The Role of Skills in Autonomy

Skills, not just savings, form the foundation of autonomy. Financial assets can erode, but skills remain portable and adaptable across industries. Developing high-value skills — such as communication, strategy, technology, or problem-solving — ensures that you can create income on your terms regardless of economic shifts. This is why skill-building often yields faster freedom than pure saving; it expands earning potential and provides control over how work is structured.

Equally important is the ability to combine skills creatively. Unique combinations — marketing expertise paired with data analysis, or financial literacy paired with design — open doors to opportunities that few others can compete in. These combinations create leverage, allowing you to charge premium rates or build ventures that require less effort for greater return.

Transitioning toward autonomy begins with restructuring finances to prioritize flexibility over distant milestones. Instead of saving exclusively for an age-based retirement target, channel resources into assets and systems that generate cash flow today. This may include building small, reliable income streams from investments, creating digital products that sell without ongoing input, or establishing service models that can be scaled or paused as needed. The emphasis shifts from accumulation to sustainability — designing income that supports freedom in the present and adapts to changing life goals.

A practical step in this shift is lowering fixed expenses without compromising quality of life. Reducing obligations like unnecessary debt or oversized housing costs frees resources that can be redirected into ventures or investments that enhance autonomy. The goal is not austerity but intentionality: spending on what aligns with your values and trimming what does not. This flexibility creates breathing room for experimentation, enabling you to test new projects or transition gradually from employment to self-directed work rather than making abrupt, risky leaps.

Purpose becomes the anchor that prevents autonomy from turning into aimlessness. Without a clear sense of direction, freedom can feel empty. Many people discover that they do not want to stop working entirely; they want to stop doing work that feels meaningless. Autonomy provides the space to pursue projects that align with personal mission, whether that involves solving problems, creating, teaching, or building something enduring. This sense of purpose transforms financial freedom into fulfillment rather than just escape.

Maintaining autonomy requires continual learning and adaptation. Markets evolve, technologies shift, and personal priorities change over time. Relying on a single strategy leaves you vulnerable; cultivating a mindset of curiosity and resilience keeps you ahead. Regularly reassess your systems, income sources, and goals to ensure they remain aligned with the life you want. What served you well five years ago may need refinement to match the person you have become.

One of the most overlooked benefits of designing autonomy is how it redefines risk. Traditional retirement planning assumes security comes from long-term employment and steady savings, yet this exposes you to risks like job loss, inflation, or sudden market downturns. Autonomy spreads risk by diversifying income and building adaptable skills, making you less dependent on any single factor. Ironically, what many perceive as risky — stepping away from rigid career paths — often creates more stability in the long run.

When viewed this way, the pursuit of autonomy is not a rejection of work but a reimagining of it. Work becomes an expression of creativity and contribution rather than a trade of time for survival. You are free to scale up during seasons of ambition and slow down during seasons of rest, without jeopardizing your future. This dynamic flexibility is the true reward: a life built around choice, where freedom is woven into every stage rather than deferred to the end.

Minimalism and Multiplication

Building wealth often feels like an exercise in addition. People accumulate possessions, commitments, and even opportunities, assuming that more is always better. Yet real growth often begins with subtraction. Minimalism, when applied intentionally, clears the noise and creates space for focus. Multiplication, on the other hand, happens when what remains is directed with precision and compounded over time. Together, these two principles form a powerful framework for achieving both financial and personal freedom.

Why Less Creates More

The modern economy constantly pushes consumption. Social media highlights lifestyles defined by abundance, while traditional advice equates success with visible accumulation. This mindset leads to clutter — not just physical, but mental and financial. Multiple income streams, subscriptions, and projects can feel productive yet quietly drain energy. Without clarity, opportunities compete for attention, and effort becomes diluted.

Minimalism cuts through this clutter by asking what truly matters. It does not mean deprivation or asceticism; it means stripping away the unnecessary to concentrate on what delivers the greatest return in life and finances. By removing distractions, minimalism sharpens focus. This focus is what makes multiplication possible, allowing resources and energy to concentrate on fewer, higher-impact actions rather than being spread thin.

The Multiplication Effect

Multiplication is the natural outcome of compounding. When effort, capital, or skill is applied consistently in the right direction, growth accelerates. This is visible in investing, where returns on reinvested gains create exponential curves, but it also applies to personal development and business. Skills compound when layered; relationships deepen over time; systems improve as they are refined. The principle is simple: what you nurture multiplies.

Minimalism and multiplication work together by ensuring that only the most valuable elements are multiplied. Without minimalism, people often multiply noise — more commitments, more distractions, more unprofitable ventures. With minimalism, the few high-leverage priorities receive full attention, accelerating results while reducing stress.

Identifying High-Value Priorities

Applying these principles begins with ruthless clarity about what creates the greatest impact. This might mean focusing on one business model instead of juggling several, or investing in a single skill that unlocks multiple opportunities rather than chasing unrelated certifications. Many individuals underestimate the cost of divided attention; each additional project not only requires time but also fragments focus, slowing progress on all fronts.

To identify high-value priorities, examine both impact and alignment. Impact measures potential returns — financial, personal, or relational. Alignment measures how closely an opportunity fits your strengths and long-term vision. The sweet spot lies where high impact meets strong alignment. These are the areas where minimalism should focus and multiplication should occur.

Implementing minimalism effectively begins with a process of elimination. Audit commitments, expenses, and goals, questioning which truly contribute to long-term vision. Many people discover they are carrying obligations out of habit rather than necessity. Cutting these creates immediate bandwidth — mental and financial — that can be redirected toward priorities with the highest leverage. This step alone often leads to noticeable momentum, as energy once scattered begins to converge.

Once distractions are removed, the next step is refinement. Concentrate resources on fewer, better opportunities. For example, instead of diversifying into multiple small side hustles with modest returns, focus on scaling one that has proven potential. Rather than spreading investments across random options, deepen understanding in one asset class and execute with precision. Multiplication occurs not through chasing variety but by deepening mastery and compounding results in areas that matter most.

Systems play a critical role in sustaining this approach. Minimalism simplifies inputs, but without structure, even a lean strategy can unravel. Build frameworks that ensure consistency — habits for saving and reinvesting, workflows for maintaining focus, and checkpoints for reviewing progress. These systems reduce reliance on willpower and transform aligned actions into effortless routines. Over time, this consistency allows compounding to accelerate with minimal friction.

A key mindset shift is recognizing that minimalism is not about doing less for its own sake but creating space for more meaningful multiplication. Eliminating clutter makes room for creativity, strategic thinking, and rest, all of which enhance performance. The result is a life where progress feels lighter, not heavier, and where each new layer of growth builds on a solid foundation rather than adding chaos.

As multiplication takes hold, results often arrive faster than expected. Small daily optimizations in finances, habits, or skills begin to intersect and amplify each other. A refined skill leads to a better opportunity, which leads to increased income, which fuels reinvestment into personal growth, creating a cycle of upward momentum. What once required relentless effort begins to feel natural and sustainable.

This balance between minimalism and multiplication ultimately leads to a quieter kind of abundance. It is not the loud accumulation of possessions or constant hustle but the steady expansion of choice and capability. Life simplifies even as impact grows. The reward is not only financial freedom but also clarity and peace — knowing that every action taken aligns with what matters most and multiplies into something greater over time.

Building Wealth That Can't Be Taken Away

Most people equate wealth with numbers in a bank account, properties they own, or investments they hold. While these can be valuable, they are also vulnerable. Markets crash, currencies inflate, governments change laws, and circumstances outside personal control can erode what once felt secure. True wealth is not only measured by financial assets but by the skills, relationships, and internal resources that remain regardless of external conditions. This deeper kind of wealth is what creates resilience and enduring freedom.

The Fragility of External Assets

Financial markets reward preparation but punish complacency. Relying entirely on a single stream of income or one asset class exposes you to risk. A company can close, industries can decline, and even well-diversified investments can be hit by unexpected global events. Many who seemed wealthy during economic booms find themselves scrambling when downturns arrive because their version of wealth depended entirely on circumstances they did not control.

This does not mean abandoning financial assets. It means understanding their limits and pairing them with forms of wealth that cannot be stolen or diminished by market cycles. When you combine tangible assets with intangible ones, you create a level of security that no single crisis can undo.

Skill-Based Wealth

Skills are among the most durable forms of wealth. Once acquired, they cannot be confiscated, and they adapt to new environments and opportunities. A person skilled in communication, negotiation, or problem-solving can generate value in any economy. Technical abilities, such as coding, marketing, or design, remain portable even when industries shift. The combination of multiple skills — especially when they intersect in unique ways — creates advantages competitors cannot easily replicate.

Developing these skills is a lifelong process, and the investment compounds. Each skill learned builds on existing abilities, opening doors that were previously invisible. Over time, this accumulation forms a personal "portfolio" of capabilities that generates income opportunities regardless of external changes.

Relationship Capital

Another form of wealth often overlooked is the network of relationships built over time. Trust, credibility, and mutual respect create opportunities that money alone cannot buy. A strong network provides access to insights, partnerships, and support during challenges. In times of uncertainty, relationships often provide the bridge to new ventures, markets, or solutions when formal systems fail.

Cultivating relationship capital requires more than collecting contacts. It involves consistently creating value for others, maintaining integrity, and nurturing connections without expectation of immediate return. Over years, these relationships compound in the same way financial investments do, producing benefits that extend far beyond transactions.

Building enduring wealth also involves cultivating the mindset that can navigate uncertainty without panic. Mental resilience allows you to respond to setbacks as temporary rather than permanent, turning challenges into opportunities for growth rather than reasons to retreat. People who develop this inner stability approach financial turbulence with creativity and calm, seeking solutions while others freeze. This composure becomes an invisible asset, protecting decision-making during critical moments.

Balancing tangible and intangible assets is key. Financial investments provide stability and opportunities for growth, but they must be paired with continual self-development. Allocating time and resources to learning, networking, and health creates a foundation that magnifies the returns on traditional wealth. A strong skillset enhances the ability to grow income; good health ensures you can pursue opportunities fully; trusted relationships open doors that money alone cannot access. Each form of wealth reinforces the others, creating a resilient ecosystem rather than a single point of failure. Practical steps to strengthen this balance include setting aside consistent time for learning high-value skills, building savings as a buffer rather than a finish line, and approaching networking as an exchange of value rather than a transaction. The intention is to create a life where income streams, knowledge, and relationships evolve together. This approach reduces dependency on any one factor and ensures adaptability as circumstances shift.

Protecting what cannot be taken away also requires clarity of personal values. Without this clarity, wealth can become a trap, leading to the pursuit of external markers of success that do not align with inner fulfillment. When you know what truly matters, it becomes easier to resist distractions and focus on building resources that support that vision. This alignment prevents the cycle of chasing more for its own sake and ensures that the wealth you build serves a meaningful purpose.

Over time, this layered approach transforms the way you experience security. Instead of relying solely on volatile markets or external conditions, you draw confidence from the skills, relationships, and perspective you have cultivated. External success may fluctuate, but your ability to generate value and create opportunities remains constant. This is the essence of wealth that cannot be taken away — not just assets on paper, but the enduring capacity to adapt, contribute, and thrive no matter what changes around you.

Chapter 12: The Money Untold Essence Blueprint

Integrating Mindset, Skills, and Strategy

Wealth creation often fails not because people lack effort, but because their approach is fragmented. They focus on building skills but neglect mindset, or they adopt strategies without the foundation to execute them effectively. Sustainable success emerges when these three elements — mindset, skills, and strategy — are aligned and reinforcing each other. Each acts as a multiplier for the others: strong skills are limited without the right mindset, mindset alone cannot replace execution, and strategy provides direction so effort compounds instead of scattering.

The Role of Mindset in Execution

Mindset is the lens through which opportunities and challenges are interpreted. A scarcity mindset sees risk in every move and hesitates to act. An abundance mindset views challenges as temporary and focuses on possibilities. This distinction shapes every decision, from how you invest time and money to how you respond to setbacks. Without a growth-oriented mindset, skills remain underutilized and strategies never fully deployed.

Cultivating this mindset involves reframing failure as feedback rather than as evidence of inadequacy. When you treat missteps as data, they refine your approach instead of discouraging progress. This shift does not eliminate discomfort but transforms it into a sign of growth. Over time, it creates resilience — a core advantage in environments where uncertainty is the norm.

Skills as Multipliers

Skills turn potential into results. They provide the tools to execute strategies and adapt to changing conditions. High-value skills — negotiation, problem-solving, communication, and technical proficiency — are particularly powerful because they apply across industries and compound when combined. Someone who understands finance and storytelling can influence investors and customers alike. A person skilled in systems thinking and leadership can scale ventures efficiently while maintaining cohesion.

Acquiring these skills requires deliberate practice rather than passive consumption. Reading about negotiation is different from applying it in real scenarios; studying marketing differs from running campaigns and analyzing results. The compound effect appears when each skill builds on the others, creating unique combinations that competitors cannot easily replicate.

Strategy as the Unifying Force

Without a coherent strategy, even strong skills and resilient mindset risk becoming wasted effort. Strategy provides clarity on where to direct energy, how to allocate resources, and what milestones matter most. It distinguishes between urgent tasks and impactful actions, ensuring progress moves toward long-term goals rather than short-term distractions.

A strong strategy also integrates feedback loops. Rather than rigid plans that crumble under change, effective strategies evolve as new information emerges. This adaptability allows for course corrections without losing momentum, preserving the benefits of consistency while remaining responsive to reality.

Aligning mindset, skills, and strategy begins with an honest assessment of where you are strong and where gaps exist. Many individuals overestimate one area and neglect another — for example, accumulating skills without building the belief to use them, or adopting ambitious strategies without the capabilities to execute. A clear inventory helps prioritize what needs development first, preventing wasted effort and accelerating measurable progress.

Creating this alignment is most effective when approached as an iterative process rather than a one-time fix. Start by clarifying the end vision: not just a financial target, but the lifestyle and values you want to sustain. With that clarity, select the skills most likely to move you toward that vision and design strategies around those capabilities. As you gain experience, feedback from real-world results informs both mindset and strategic direction, closing gaps and strengthening weak points.

Daily habits form the bridge that keeps these elements connected. A strategy only works if consistently acted upon; skills improve through repetition;

mindset is reinforced through daily wins and the reflection that follows setbacks. Small routines — reviewing key metrics, setting intentions, practicing a skill in real scenarios — anchor the larger framework in tangible actions. Over months, these habits compound, creating visible progress that fuels confidence and reinforces the cycle.

Feedback loops are essential. A growth-oriented mindset looks for lessons in every outcome, using them to refine both skills and strategies. Regular reflection, whether weekly or monthly, provides space to ask crucial questions: Did this approach work as intended? Where did I hesitate, and why? Which skills need deeper refinement to unlock the next level of results? This rhythm prevents stagnation and ensures continued evolution, even as goals shift.

Integration also requires intentional exposure to environments that challenge and expand you. Surrounding yourself with peers and mentors who embody the results you seek accelerates growth by modeling behaviors, offering perspective, and holding you accountable to higher standards. These relationships not only sharpen skills and strategies but also reinforce mindset, normalizing ambition and resilience rather than isolation or self-doubt.

When these three elements function together, they create momentum that feels self-sustaining. Strategy channels focus, skills deliver execution, and mindset fuels persistence. Progress accelerates not because external conditions become easier, but because internal alignment removes friction. The pursuit of wealth and autonomy stops feeling fragmented and starts to feel inevitable — not in the sense of entitlement, but in the quiet confidence that comes from knowing every part of you is moving in the same direction.

90-Day Wealth Recalibration Plan

A full financial transformation can feel overwhelming, but ninety days is long enough to create visible results without feeling impossible. This time frame allows you to build momentum, reset habits, and lay the groundwork for lasting change. The focus is not on extreme sacrifices or overnight riches, but on recalibrating your approach to money so that your actions, mindset, and goals align. At the end of ninety days, you will not only see measurable improvements but also feel more control over your financial direction.

Laying the Foundation: Clarity and Baseline

The first step is clarity. Without knowing your current position, every decision will be reactive rather than strategic. Begin by taking inventory of your financial reality — income, expenses, debt, savings, and investments. This process is not about judgment but awareness. Many people avoid looking at their full picture out of fear, yet understanding the baseline is empowering. It turns vague stress into specific numbers, which can be managed and improved.

Once you have this baseline, define what success would look like ninety days from now. This might include building an emergency fund, paying down a specific amount of debt, or creating a new source of income. Goals should be ambitious enough to inspire effort but realistic enough to accomplish in the time frame. Clarity on both your current position and desired outcome provides a roadmap for the next steps.

Mindset Reset: Breaking Scarcity Patterns

Financial recalibration begins in the mind. Scarcity thinking — the belief that opportunities are limited and setbacks are permanent — leads to short-term decisions and chronic stress. Rewiring this pattern involves reframing money as a tool rather than a source of fear. Simple daily practices, such as gratitude for existing resources or visualization of future outcomes, help shift focus from lack to possibility. This shift is critical because strategies only work when you believe change is possible.

Mindset work also includes redefining your relationship with work and value. Instead of viewing income as strictly tied to hours worked, start recognizing the link between value created and rewards received. This perspective opens doors to leverage and opportunities that linear thinking often overlooks.

Strategic Simplification

With clarity and mindset aligned, the next phase is simplifying your financial landscape. Complexity drains energy and hides inefficiencies. Reduce scattered accounts, cancel unused subscriptions, and consolidate debt where possible. Simplification does not mean inaction; it creates space for focused execution. A clean structure makes it easier to track progress and spot areas for improvement during the next ninety days.

At this stage, choose one or two key priorities rather than attempting to fix everything at once. For many, this might be stabilizing cash flow or eliminating a major source of financial leakage. Concentrated effort on a few priorities produces faster wins, which builds confidence and fuels continued momentum.

The recalibration gains strength through structured rhythms that create consistency without overwhelming you. Weekly reviews are a key anchor. At the end of each week, reflect on income generated, expenses managed, and any actions that moved you closer to your priority goal. This regular checkpoint ensures that small deviations are corrected quickly rather than compounding into major setbacks. It also reinforces the connection between daily effort and tangible results, which is vital for maintaining motivation over three months.

Daily habits form the backbone of the plan. Simple routines, such as tracking every expense for awareness or dedicating thirty focused minutes to skill development, produce measurable shifts over time. These habits should align with the highest-impact priorities identified earlier. If building cash flow is your focus, daily outreach or product development takes precedence. If stabilizing finances is the goal, reviewing spending patterns and making intentional adjustments becomes non-negotiable. By narrowing focus, you reduce decision fatigue and direct energy where it matters most.

Midway through the ninety days, evaluate your progress and adjust strategies as needed. This midpoint is not a pass-or-fail moment but a chance to refine. If a tactic is not producing results, replace it rather than abandoning the entire plan. Flexibility ensures momentum continues even when circumstances shift. Many breakthroughs occur in the second half of the plan, when new habits solidify and compounding effects begin to show.

Celebrating small wins is as important as setting ambitious targets. A paid-off credit card, a first client secured, or a week of consistent saving signals that the system is working. These milestones build belief and reinforce the behaviors that created them. Acknowledging progress also prevents burnout by shifting attention from how far you still have to go toward how much you have already achieved.

As the ninety days conclude, the focus moves from short-term actions to integration. The gains achieved — clearer financial awareness, new habits, improved cash flow — must be embedded into a sustainable framework. Create a simple system to maintain weekly reviews, continue skill development, and plan quarterly recalibrations. This ensures the process does not end with the ninety days but evolves into an ongoing cycle of refinement and growth.

By the end of this period, the transformation is more than numerical. Beyond any increase in income or reduction in debt, you will have built a foundation of clarity, resilience, and control over your financial path. The recalibration shifts money management from reactive to intentional, positioning you to pursue bigger opportunities with confidence and focus. This is the quiet but profound power of a deliberate ninety-day reset: it changes not only your finances but the way you approach wealth creation for the rest of your life.

Living the Code Daily

The real test of transformation is not what you know but what you do consistently. A powerful mindset or strategy loses impact without daily application. Living the code means embodying the principles of wealth, autonomy, and focus until they become second nature. This is less about rigid discipline and more about creating an environment and routines that naturally align with the person you are becoming.

Anchoring Identity Through Action

True change begins with identity. When you see yourself as someone who manages money intentionally, makes decisions strategically, and prioritizes growth, your actions naturally follow. Identity-based habits are more durable than motivation-based ones because they align with who you believe yourself to be. Each small action — reviewing your numbers, learning a new skill, or choosing a high-value task over distraction — is a vote for the identity you are building.

Shifting identity requires conscious reinforcement. Remind yourself daily of the person you are becoming rather than the circumstances you are leaving behind. Visual cues, such as written affirmations or a clear workspace, can reinforce this shift. Over time, the gap between who you were and who you are closes, and the behaviors that once felt forced become effortless.

Designing an Environment That Supports the Code

Environment often shapes behavior more than willpower. A cluttered desk or constant notifications can undermine even the strongest intentions. Living the code daily begins with designing surroundings that reduce friction for good habits and increase friction for bad ones. This may mean simplifying your financial tools, removing unnecessary digital distractions, or creating dedicated spaces for focused work and reflection.

A supportive environment also includes people. Surrounding yourself with individuals who share similar goals accelerates growth and makes the code feel normal rather than exceptional. The right conversations challenge complacency and reinforce commitment. Over time, community becomes a multiplier, turning personal growth into collective momentum.

Aligning Daily Decisions With Long-Term Vision

Everyday decisions, even seemingly small ones, accumulate into long-term outcomes. The code acts as a filter: does this choice move me closer to autonomy, or does it reinforce dependence? Does it build skills and assets, or does it drain time and energy? These micro-decisions — what to spend on, what to learn, where to invest effort — create the trajectory of your financial and personal life.

Clarity of vision simplifies these choices. When you know what you are building toward, decisions stop feeling like sacrifices and start feeling like alignment. Skipping a short-term indulgence or dedicating an evening to skill development becomes natural because it fits the larger picture you are committed to.

Momentum builds when principles become rituals rather than occasional efforts. Morning routines that combine mental focus, financial review, and skill practice set the tone for the day ahead. Even ten minutes spent clarifying priorities or tracking key numbers reinforces the mindset of intentional control. These rituals should feel supportive rather than burdensome, anchoring you to the code without adding unnecessary complexity.

Sustainability matters more than intensity. Many people start strong but burn out because their approach is unrealistic. A sustainable rhythm respects energy levels and recognizes that consistency compounds more than sporadic bursts of effort. Choosing one or two high-impact habits and maintaining them daily creates more change than chasing perfection. Over weeks, these consistent actions rewire patterns and prove that transformation is not dependent on willpower alone.

Adversity provides the ultimate test of living the code. It is easy to follow principles when circumstances are ideal, but growth happens in moments of stress or setback. Challenges expose which habits are truly ingrained and which are surface-level. Meeting these moments with reflection rather than reaction strengthens resilience. Instead of abandoning the code, use difficulties as feedback to refine it. This approach transforms obstacles into opportunities for deeper mastery.

Integrating reflection into the daily rhythm ensures that growth remains intentional. Brief evening reviews — identifying what worked, what felt misaligned, and what can be adjusted tomorrow — create continuous improvement without self-criticism. Over time, these reflections reveal patterns: recurring distractions, consistent wins, and areas for skill development. Awareness grows, and with it, the ability to make precise adjustments rather than vague resolutions.

As the code becomes embodied, external results begin to reflect internal alignment. Financial stability improves, opportunities appear, and decision-making feels clearer. Yet the true reward lies in the sense of agency. Living by design rather than default transforms wealth-building from a distant pursuit into a daily practice. Each choice, no matter how small, becomes a step toward autonomy and a life shaped on your terms.

Ultimately, the code is not something you complete. It evolves with you, adapting as your goals and circumstances change. What remains constant is the commitment to deliberate living — a refusal to drift and a dedication to creating value in every area of life. When the principles are lived daily, they become less about discipline and more about identity, allowing growth to continue long after the initial motivation has faded.

Last Words

Reading changes nothing unless it turns into action.
Before you close this book, choose one principle, one shift, one step, and begin today.
Wealth starts quietly, inside you. Let it grow louder in the life you're about to build.

www.ingramcontent.com/pod-product-compliance
Lightning Source LLC
Chambersburg PA
CBHW072154160426
43197CB00012B/2386